Finding a Voice

DAMIAN QUINN

Cover design by Book Beaver Ltd
Interior design by Wordzworth Ltd
Cover Photo, (current me) by Ben Martin
Cover Photo, (younger me) by John Quinn

Technical Editor: D. V. M Bishop FRS FBA FMedSci

Printed by Kindle Direct Publishing
First Printing, 2019

ISBN 978-1-5272-2114-7

Contact: info@dysphasia.co.uk
www.dysphasia.co.uk

All the women in my life who have helped me through my life –
especially, my Mother, Theresa Quinn

Contents

Foreword   9

Preface   11

Acknowledgements   15

Introduction   17

Chapter 1   A Cry in the Night   21

Chapter 2   Mid-teens   59

Chapter 3   Family life   67

Chapter 4   Mid-twenties   73

Chapter 5   Early Thirties   77

Chapter 6   University Life   83

Chapter 7   After University   103

Chapter 8   Courses with QA   113

Chapter 9   Married life   117

Chapter 10   A Newspaper called The Early Times   137

Chapter 11   Spreading Awareness   143

Chapter 12   All about Afasic   147

Chapter 13   Vice President of Afasic   157

Chapter 14   Future Thoughts   165

References   171

Useful Information   175

Foreword

This is a very special book: as far as I know, it is the only autobiography written by someone with Developmental Language Disorder (DLD). There's a good reason for that: DLD is a disability that specifically affects the ability to communicate, whether by writing or speaking. So getting your thoughts down on paper is challenging if you have DLD: you have to cope with problems in finding the right words and expressing your thoughts in grammatical sentences, and as you struggle to get the ideas written down, your memory for what you want to say may evaporate.

I have studied DLD throughout a long research career, and I think I have some idea of what it must be like: I've sometimes explained it to people by asking them to imagine what it would be like if they had to live and work in a country where they had only a basic grasp of the language. You will often get a general idea of what people are saying, but it's hard work, and sometimes you get unstuck because you try to make sense of something on the basis of picking out a few key words. And when you have to express yourself, you know what you want to say but get frustrated at not being able to find the right words and put them in the right order. But I can't ever really understand what it is like to experience DLD, and this is why this book is so important in giving a first-hand account by a man who has lived his life with this condition.

One thing that came across from Damian's account is that language problems don't just affect ability to function in the here and now; they also have an impact on formation of long-term memories. Damian reports the contrast between himself and his wife in their ability to remember events from childhood. There is a whole branch of psychology concerned with autobiographical memory which has always interested me, because there is some evidence that language is important for laying down long-term representations of events in memory. I'd always wondered if this might explain why most of us can't remember events from very early in life. Damian's account fits this view, and suggests that if a child has DLD, then this may make their memories of childhood particularly fragile, because they find it harder to verbalise their experiences.

Another strong theme that emerges from the book is Damian's persistence and resilience in the face of repeated setbacks. If you have DLD, it affects so many aspects of life. Things that most of us may find pretty straightforward – reading, writing, socialising – can't be taken for granted. I was at times reminded of the story of the spider that was observed by Robert the Bruce repeatedly attempting to swing from one beam to another and failing. It tried, and failed, and tried again, and failed again, over and over. But eventually it got there, inspiring the Scottish King not to give up his battle against the English. Damian has shown that if you don't give up, you can make a success of life, despite a disability like DLD. In a range of roles he has found a niche where he can use his talents, most notably in helping others with similar problems. Having been effective as a Disabled Students' Officer at University, he is now a Vice-President of Afasic, where he engages in public speaking to spread the word about DLD, which is still a relatively unknown condition.

DLD is very much a hidden disability. Recognition of DLD is growing, but it will be some time before there is public awareness that this is a lifelong condition, which affects many adults who just exist beneath the radar. I hope that Damian's account of life with DLD will encourage others to make their voices heard, and lead to wider recognition and acceptance of the needs of adults with DLD, and the contribution they can make to society.

DOROTHY BISHOP, FRS, FMEDSCI, FBA
SEPTEMBER 2019

Preface

Afasic is a unique organisation and one I came to know and become CEO of via Elizabeth Browning. Elizabeth, who was Chair from 1973 to 1987, was the parent of a young adult with developmental language disorder (DLD). Afasic is unique in that it was started by a speech and language therapist, Margaret Greene, in 1967, but handed over as soon as possible to a parent to run as a parent-led organisation in the belief that parents should be given a significant role in representing and speaking up for their children. Afasic remains true to its roots today, in that it is still parent led, whilst working closely with professionals.

As CEO from 1987 to 1999 I had responsibility for continuing to organise the activity weeks started by Elizabeth Browning as a respite for the parents and a challenge and confidence-builder for the children and young people. It was through visiting these weeks that I got to know a number of them, one of whom was Damian. He was but a youngster at the time, but the man was visible as he rose to the challenges presented with relish – abseiling, potholing, climbing and more. When we were looking for young adults to talk about their experiences growing up with DLD and to act as ambassadors for the organisation he was a natural choice with his easy charm and cheeky sense of humour. He did us proud and I know his mother was immensely proud of him too. I was fortunate to get to know her well during her time as Chair of Afasic.

She, like all those who have contact with children and young people with DLD, understood that Damian was like every other young person of his age – the same desires to socialise, participate and challenge himself but with a vulnerability and a misreading by many of his capabilities and intellectual level. If you cannot communicate well via the spoken word you can be cut off cruelly from social interaction and so much of what the majority of us take for granted. It can be difficult to listen and work things out at the same time. At school, children who cannot follow long and complex instructions may be mislabelled as inattentive, naughty or stupid and the teacher may have moved on by the time a child has processed information and is ready to answer. Bullying is not uncommon and particular difficulties may be faced when having to deal with legal or other official matters

As Brian Patten, Liverpool poet, wrote for Afasic's first International Symposium:

> *I'm seven, and I'm dead bright*
> *But words give me a fright*
> *Words are bullies*
> *Sneaky things. They lie.*
> *Sometimes trying to understand them*
> *Makes me cry. Words hurt.*
> *Words are all over the place*
> *They get shoved in my face.*
> *I don't know why but*
> *Words make me cry.*

EXTRACT FROM 'WORDS' BY BRIAN PATTEN – NOW RENAMED 'APHASIA'

Damian was one of the lucky ones in that, as he described in his story, he went to a special school for those with language difficulties. But nonetheless he has had to face many challenges and hardships, which he has done with fortitude and courage and in numerous ways overcome.

And he has now provided us with, for the first time, a personal account of what it can be like growing up with DLD. Elizabeth Browning in 1972 wrote 'I can't see what you're saying' (now sadly out of print) about her experiences as a mother proving solace for other mothers in her position. Damian's story helps us to understand the world from his perspective, to understand he is like the rest of us and to not jump to conclusions about why someone might have difficulty in understanding and responding to what they are saying.

For myself, I count it a privilege to have got to know and work with parents, children and young adults with DLD and wouldn't have wanted to have missed it for the world.

Norma Corkish, BSc FRSA

September 2019

Acknowledgements

Writing a book about yourself isn't easy, especially when your childhood memories aren't very clear. I want to thank my wife, Libby, for sticking by me while I write this book and not to getting annoyed when I ask her to proof-read, even after a long day at work. Without her guidance, I couldn't have written this book.

I would also like to give a big thank you to Andrea, for making me smile every time I see her with her love of humour and love of life and being my sister. You mean a lot to me.

I also should thank my Mother, for believing in me, having faith in me, giving me confidence, and not getting so stressed out when I didn't work hard enough in my studies. She is the key reason I have the motivation to write this book.

I also would like to thank my friend, Kim, for making me smile whenever she chats to me and taking time out to learn about what Speech, Language, and Communications Needs are and teaching me that not all mainstream people are bad.

I want to thank the team at Afasic but in particular Linda Lascelles. Without you guys, I wouldn't have had the confidence to become Vice President for the charity, or the opportunity to spread awareness of such a brilliant charity. You guys mean lots to me.

If I didn't have my tutors at School, College and University, I wouldn't have found my passion for IT and Web Development. These tutors gave me the understanding and the resources to work like mad on my computer, learning and building the website that accompanies this autobiography.

Although I was a troublemaker at Dawn House School, I must thank Marion, my house parent and all the staff at my school for believing in me. I hope I didn't cause you all to go out of your mind too much.

I would also like to thank everyone who I met at University, students and tutors alike. They have been making me laugh and making me enjoy the world that I live in nowadays.

And finally, I need to thank you, the readers, for buying this book. Without the reader, the awareness of the disability that is explained in this book would never get explained, or the awareness spread across the globe. I can't spread awareness without your help, or the help from my readers telling other people about the autobiography, so I will hope that you will tell everyone you know about this and the book gets noticed.

Introduction

I breathed my first breath, booted up the laptop and opened up Microsoft Word. What was I going to write? How am I going to write about it? This was going to be a book that would breathe life into my words. I was scared, but I recognised that it needed to be done.

I breathed again and started typing. It was difficult and at some points, upsetting to me as I remembered my childhood. I keep typing, and after a long while, I finished the first page – the title of the book!

In the thought of Col. Hans Landa from *Inglorious Basterds*: "Oooer…isn't this exciting? I am writing my first book!"

I'm sorry, I should introduce myself as you may be wondering who I am — Hello, and welcome to my madcap of a life. My name is Damo, and I'm the author of this book. I have written this autobiography to spread awareness of my disability, DLD, and to show you how I have coped with the disability. I hope to show you the sadness of the disability, as well as the good through my writings. I also have brought some interesting topics to this book. In Chapter 1: What is DLD, I decided to include lots of psychology papers to talk about what Developmental Learning Disorder (DLD) is, and I want to explain why I use the word 'Dysphasia' in some areas and DLD in other areas, it happens to be the largest part of the book.

"Why have I decided to write this?" you may well be asking. Well, over the years, I have felt that my disability hasn't quite got the publicity that it deserves. Yes, there has been research into it, but not enough. I also think that this is my view of the disability and how it affects me. So, I would like to show you the world through my eyes, not you read it from a professional who knows about the disability but doesn't know how it affects the world around the person who has the disability.

Like with everyone, I have been knocked down, but as *Thomas*

J Watson, the CEO of International Business Machines (IBM) once said:

> *"If you stand up and be counted, from time to time, you may get yourself knocked down. But remember this: A man flattened by an opponent can get up again. A man flattened by conformity stays down for good."*

That's what I have done. I got back up and soldiered on through life, ever moulding myself to be what I am today.

I am always thankful for the opportunities that I have got in life, and the biggest reward that I received was to be a Vice-President of a national charity that is called Afasic. This Charity supports children, young adults and their families with Developmental Language Disorder (DLD) or as I call it, dysphasia. It is a small charity with a very big heart, as it works hard to spread awareness, as well as helping all the members who have DLD. I have been working for them for 26 years, doing talks and attending events, and am continuing to spread awareness by writing this book, my website and other media sources. I will talk more about Afasic later in the autobiography.

I had met some wonderful people throughout my life who had become my friends, such as when I went to University in Derby. I am very honoured that I have gained the friends, and couldn't do without them as they have helped me through the later part of my life and helped me see that this disability is a part of me, but doesn't define who I am. It hasn't been easy, but I have finally got to a place in life where I am happy. Lots of remembering what I was like and adapting to change myself for the better. I must always remember this though – '*Friends come, friends go, but only the true friends stay*', which is a quote from me in the early noughties. I wouldn't say no to having the quote linked to me, like the famous quotes of Winston Churchill, Julius Caesar or Shakespeare.

Away from all of this, I do enjoy my learning and socialising. I hope that I can show you this within the confines of this book. I have built a website from scratch using HTML5, CSS3, JavaScript, and Bootstrap. I've used tutorial videos as well as books and online books to get it where it is now. I will continue to build on it as time goes on and make it even better. I am also wanting to continue to learn to make myself better in other areas of I.T., such as building my computer, which is very fast and powerful. In other areas of my life, I'd like to see myself build on my life in general, like for example, learning new things such as languages (computer), British Sign Language.

So, without further ado, as Dylan Thomas puts it in his play 'Under the Milkwood'[1] and read so wonderfully by Richard Burton for the BBC: '*To begin at the beginning*'. I should start right there – the beginning in this swashbuckling tale of my life…no, I'm just joking…not swashbuckling but 'Don't try this at home' kind of tale…

CHAPTER 1

A Cry in the Night

*The development of the language is part of the development of
the personality, for words are the natural means of expressing
thoughts and establishing understanding between people*

—MARIA MONTESSORI

Winter 1974. Somewhere in a town in the United Kingdom.

It's a cold, dark night. The wind is whistling all-around a house, and
its cold icy breath stops any animal or insect to coming out and playing
under the silvery light of the cold moon. Look there, and something is
moving. Two silhouettes that the moon cannot even light up, scurrying
along a small path, hunched over with steam appearing every minute
along to a waiting car. An American voice says, 'The hospital please, and
fast'. The car groans to life and the tires spins into actions against the
snow trodden road, and it trundles off into the night, complaining. The
streetlights are the only thing that is seeing in that dark, miserable cold
night as the moon has gone away to somewhere warmer.

The streets are clear, and the car races past streetlights that turn into
orange snakes that look at the little car and decide to race it. The man

looks at the woman and says 'Please remember to do what the midwife told us, breath. One, two, three, one, two, thre-...' the woman shouts 'YOU'RE NOT HELPING!'. The man gives the order to move faster, and the car starts to beat the race between itself and the orange snakes.

Finally, the car arrives at the hospital and it screeches to a halt after it drifted into parking space as if it was trying out for a stunt in a Hollywood blockbuster and the two people get out, and the woman is greeted by the nurses and taken off into the hospital. The man scurries worriedly into the hospital following his wife and the party of anxious nurses.

"You stay here, Sir." ordered the nurses "but I am the hus-..." replied the man and the door shuts in his face "...band" he finishes off to the big grey cold door who looks at him coldly.

The hallway that the man paces in is a cold and uninviting hallway with grey walls and poorly taken photographs from the yesteryear hung with sadness as if they had seen all that passed them. It smells of bleach and stale blood. It is dimly lit, and the man notices that one of the lights is winking at him. He gives it a tap, but it just buzzes at him and then continues to wink at him. This is the only light is that is working. Down the walls, there is water stains and old dusty cobwebs that entwine with each other. He listens out for every sound and watching everyone who scurried in and out of the room, like mice hunting out cheese with the words "Not yet". A little spider scampers across the wall. The man looks at her. "Bet you're never this worried when you have your babies," he says. The spider looks at him, and then continues on her journey as if to say, "Don't have time for this."

At the stroke of the hour, a cry came out of the room and the cold door that stopped the man from going in, squeaked into action, and an excited nurse ran out of the room. She was dull looking, dressed in a grey uniform with dirty grey, white hair as if it hasn't been washed for years. She looked around and saw the man pacing. In her best lively voice, she exclaims excitedly "Mr Quinn, Mr Quinn; you can go in now. She's given birth to a beautiful baby boy. You should be pleased." But the words only come out as a dull and boring sentence. He rushes in not caring if the nurse gets hurt or not, "yes I am" he replies as he pushes past the nurse.

He goes to the bed and sees the woman holding a baby. She looks at her husband, "Meet your son, John. I want to call him Damian." She says, "That is a good name, Theresa" he replies.

I was born in February 1974 at 10 pm to two happy parents, John and Theresa Quinn. My parents were working-class people who worked hard. My father is an American who, in 1968, came to London as an Animation student, where he met my Mother through my uncle. I will leave my dad to tell the story of how he and my Mother got together. His bit comes afterwards. Anyway, my Mother worked for an organisation that built and installed memorials into the graveyards of the churches and throughout her career, she travelled all over the UK and Europe. She started as a secretary and then after a few years she moved into the role of CEO. During this time, she had me, and both she and my dad was pleased that everything went well during birth. Unfortunately, it wasn't until two years afterwards that they realised that I couldn't speak at all.

My father was a photographer for a famous auction house in London.

I asked my father to write a bit of the autobiography, and he kindly accepted. Here are his words:

"At the age of 26, I came to England in 1968 to attend classes at the London School of Film, where I met and became good friends with Ron. Later through him and his wife, Meryl, I met Theresa and her family. I liked her very much.

"Later, in 1970, while I was working in Washington, D.C., I heard that Theresa got a divorce, and I returned to London the following year to see her. We got on very well, and the following year, we decided to marry. So, on June 3rd, 1972, we exchanged rings. Together with Theresa & Andrea, I found that I had gained an instant family!

"On February 20th, 1974, Damian was born, and we had gained a fourth member to the family (years later, we gained a

fifth member when a cat, Max, adopted us!). A short time after Damian's birth, I found myself unemployed, but, eventually, was employed as a staff photographer at Sotheby's (the auction house in London). I loved the work & my colleagues so much that I never left. I remained a fine arts photographer (watches, clocks, works of art, & jewellery being my main fields) there for 25 years until I retired in 2002.

"Damian was slow at walking & speaking, but Theresa & I assured ourselves that he was just a 'slow' learner and would catch up eventually. Although his speech was limited to a few words ("la" instead of "light"), we understood him — as parents do with their children — and we were heartened that all would be well when he started walking (and once he started his first steps, around 2, he progressed rapidly).

"Unfortunately, his speech (grasping abstract terms like beauty, height, north & south) was still very rudimentary, and his pronunciation gave us a reason for concern. Eventually, his grandmother, Joyce MacLaren (herself, a speech therapist) advised us to take him for speech sessions with Mary Courtman-Davis. She helped him, but even she couldn't rectify his speech to a level expected for a boy of his age, and he was, eventually, diagnosed with dysphasia.

"Around 6, for two years, he went to a small, lovely, caring local school in Hockliffe, where he made friends — despite his poor speech — but Theresa knew that he would always be behind in an ordinary school, so the search for a more suitable school began. It was a tough fight for her, with the local council trying to save money by having him enrolled in a local — and totally unsuitable — school. The struggle went on for about a year, and Theresa even had to enlist the help of her MP to get Damian into a school that could cater to his needs.

"Theresa, Damian & I went to visit life-long friends in Philadelphia in 1982, and their 8-year old son, Bobby, instantly became a great friend & constant companion for Damian, even though neither understood the other's speech of very well. They

did, however —through the mystery of osmosis— understand what the other was trying to communicate. They became so close during those two weeks that Bobby cried when Damian returned to England! But over the years, they met again & again (including a wonderful holiday at Disney World for one summer).

"Damian was enrolled at Dawn House, in Rainworth (Mansfield), at the age of 8, so that he could be with other speech-impaired children, and receive specialized education to help him overcome his handicap. He was at Dawn House until he was 16.

"Although he was a happy, popular student at the school, he loved coming home every other weekend (a 3½ hour journey each way on the M1), and when it came time to return to Rainworth, he became very stressed over leaving (which, in turn, tore out our hearts every time!), but when he arrived, and saw his friends again (and Marion, his 'house' mother), the pain eased and he settled in quickly until his next return. His six-week summer vacations were like 'heaven on earth' for us because there were NO weekends cut short by the return journey to school, and we had the time to take him places (in England and Disney World, in Florida)."

I want to thank my father for writing that for my autobiography. When I was born, my parents didn't know that I was DLD. They didn't know I had a speech and language impairment until I was about two years old. How my parents knew was by me only making sounds and no words. Fortunately, my grandmother was a speech therapist for stroke patients and had a fair idea of why I wasn't speaking properly. But she wasn't 100% sure as she only witnessed this kind of disability with people who have had a stroke in their later life. This was something new for her, but my Mother always said, she doesn't know where she'd be if she didn't have the help of my grandmother.

My grandmother was born in May 1902. During World War II (WWII), my grandmother was asked to serve her country by helping the hospitals as an ambulance driver. She would have to go out on calls every night, and during the Blitz, collecting all the injured and taking them to the hospitals to be looked after. It couldn't be easy during this time for anyone who was pregnant, but fortunately, my Mother was born in 1943 and was a bundle of joy for my grandmother. After the war, she became a speech therapist for the victims of stroke. Like with me, these patients that she received had the loss of speech through brain damage of some description, but instead of being born with it, they were adults when they were hit with the disability. Also, she taught Arabic to a small class in her home.

Every year on her birthday, she drove my Mother up the wall by going off to Greece for a 2-week holiday. The reason why it drove my Mother up the wall was that we needed to celebrate her birthday before she left. This happened every year up to when my grandmother was 86 years old.

She was fit as a fiddle, as she lived in a house which was the Victorian times where it was 4 storeys (basement, ground floor, first floor, attic – the attic she had lodgers living in it for a time) and the stairs between the basement (which was the kitchen and dining room) and ground floor (the living room). Between every floor, there were steep staircases. They kept her fit, as it was like climbing a mountain to get from the kitchen to the dining room to the bedrooms. She lived in that house from the moment she bought it, in the 1930s to the day she died, aged 91. I found out recently that when she died, her house had to go back to the council as she rented it throughout her life. I had wished that we still had the house as her area has gone up in the world since she lived there. When my grandmother lived there, my Mother drove herself and me to my grandmother's house, and we went past Kings Cross, and we could see all the prostitutes lining the kerb. Back in the 80s, it was a very dangerous area, and now, it's quite a safe area as it's been cleaned up massively. The house now could be sold for in the region of £1,000,000. But, the family didn't get it, unfortunately.

Due to my grandmother being a speech therapist, she was able to advise my mother on further steps to get me talking. She got my mother in contact with the relevant people, as she was unable to do it herself. Also, I don't think she quite knew what was happening to me. But she referred us to a friend and colleague who spent a few years with me getting the speech enough to be able to distinguish of what

I was saying. Then, it was all down to the secondary school to get the speech near on perfect. (more about the secondary school later).

I was also born deaf in the left ear, because of a layer of skin growing over the ear canal. I had two operations to try to rectify the problem at Great Ormond Street Hospital, but unfortunately, they did not work.

This kind of deafness isn't widely known about, even by medical professionals. I have gone to doctors, where they try to look in my ears. I tell them not to bother with the left, but they try, realise there's no opening, and then are surprised, and I have to explain. In these occasions, I do think "I did tell you", but I know that there's not much point in saying anything. It's funny that doctors hardly ever take a patient's word! Sometimes, I'm surprised that they don't ask me if I want it operated on to open it up. My answer to that is "No, already been tried and it doesn't work.

The other problem with having this deafness (and in some ways, good for other people) is that behind the ear I have a scar which is very sensitive. This means if Libby (more about her later) gets bored of me, she can rub it, and it'll make me fall asleep! At times, I wish that she didn't know about it!

I had tried to get a Cochlear Implant when I was about 18 years old, but when the results came back from the hearing test, the doctor who was specialising in the hearing aid, said that there isn't enough sound going into the left ear which is enough for the Cochlear Implant. So, unfortunately, I can't have one. I think at the age of 44 years old, if a doctor contacted me from the result of this book, and said the Implant has changed, so I will be able to get it now, I think that I would turn it down. Yes, I would love to hear out of both ears as it'd be useful when I'm listening in stereo, like at the cinema, but I don't think I could get used to it. And once in, I don't think it can be reversed.

There is something called 'cross-aids' where you have a microphone on the deaf side and a hearing aid on the hearing side, and it lets you hear anything on the deaf side whichever side that may be. In the case of my deafness, I'd be able to hear anything on the left side. The problem with getting this it is a very expensive job. I'm not going

27

to say exactly how much but let me say that I can't get it on my salary. I used to have it, but it went through glasses, and now they don't make cross-aids to go through glasses. Also, now the technology has changed from analogue to digital.

Over the years, I have managed to become used to the deafness, as you would over any injury or disability if it's life-long, but the problem that people have difficulty with is that they need to be on the right side of me when they're talking to me. Otherwise, it will feel like I am ignoring them. Fortunately, it doesn't bother them after they've come to accept it.

I remember my Mother saying that if I'm walking on a road with a girl, it's always polite for the man to walk on the side of the girl where the road is. That's all okay if the road is on my left, but if it isn't then, it's no good, as we would never get anywhere as I'd have to take routes where the road is on the left and if that meant that I hit a lot of 'T' junctions that could be a lot of right turns! I think she didn't say it for long when she found out that I literally couldn't hear anything when the person was on my left!

The other problem that I have is dyspraxia, but fortunately, this only affects me when I'm tired. Mainly this affects my coordination, for example, if I have to pick up a drink, I have to guide my hand to the glass by looking directly at my hand. Like I said. Fortunately, it doesn't often happen, only once that I remember although it didn't go down very well with the people sitting at the table with me! Well, it did go down… all over them!

Early Wakeup Call: The Early Mornings Practice

In the early years of my life, I was having speech therapy throughout. I would have to get up at 06:00 hours to do practice exercises, then would get driven down to London to have speech therapy. To get me up, my parents had to bribe me with chocolate drops to practice, and we would go down to London to the speech therapist who was a friend of my grandmother's. I used not to like the M1, so my Mother had to go down the A5, which meant we had to leave earlier as the A5 was a slower route at that time, unlike it is now. During the speech therapy, the therapist got me to create the words by showing me the letter, such as the letter 'A' and create the shape of this letter with the mouth. It wasn't easy, but I eventually got it. At the same time, I had to go to a local school for early year's schooling, which I attended when I was five years old.

I went to Hockliffe Lower School at the age of 5 and left when I was about 9. I had no speech while at school. I could make sounds but couldn't put words together. One tutor at the school told my parents that I was her little chatterbox. She said, 'For a child with no speech, he sure does say a lot!'

The school had a very good headmistress called Mrs Eyles. She said to my parents when they were deciding what was to come next for me, which always stuck with my Mother:

'If you want to aim high, aim for the moon,
and you will reach the stars'

and she kept on repeating it throughout my life.

My friendship group while at home, was small and consisted of two friends who lived on the street, and weren't like me (how we communicated, is anyone's guess. But children of that age are supposed to have ways of communicating without any trouble, even if one of them can speak very well), and we saw each other all the way up to when I went off to school in Nottinghamshire. The things that we did was play 'Cowboys and Indians', play at each other's houses, have water fights (I wasn't meant to when I had just had an operation on my ear!). I don't remember if we did anything else, like football (although I know when I was at school, I didn't care much for football. I never was a 'sporty' child. I just liked sitting around chatting and using the imagination). When the ice-cream van came around during the summer months, my father always got a knock at the door from my two friends and me asking for some money. I always really liked the ice cream with the flake in it, which was called a '99'. During this time, it did cost 99 pence, but now it cost £2.00 – that's inflation for you!

I now remember that time of my life with speech, but all the evidence points to me not having any speech whatsoever. Look at what I've written here; I have told you that I had to get up early to do practice that I was given by the speech therapist down in London. I also was given speech therapy probably weekly, and my Mother said that I couldn't speak. But my mind remembers that time with me speaking as well as everyone else. So, with my Mother having a better memory of that time, I will take her word for it. I guess although I was playing with the two friends, I must have had some speech, even if it wasn't perfect or that children must not *need* much language to get along with each other.

The exercises that I did was learning the alphabet by saying it by using the alphabet phonics, like 'a for ant', 'b for bat', etc. Then shortly afterwards, my Mother read to me, and I read over her shoulder, and she'd get me to read to her, with her helping me if I got stuck. I also used flashcards to learn the words. Mother would hold one up, and then I would have to say the word out loud to learn it.

All this learning took it time, but I managed to get there.

I remember another point. One of my friends invited me round to his house (who lived on my street), and he had a fully working train set in his loft. The train set was one like the *Hornby*® train set with little locomotives, stations, and people. I went up to the hatch and watched it from the edge. With me being terrified of heights, I froze and couldn't get me down and had to call my Mother in to help me out (or I managed to come to my senses and got myself down. I can't remember which).

I have had a deep-seated fear of heights for as long as I can remember. It is caused by me only being able to hear on one side. The ears, apart from being able to allow sounds in, helps with balance and with me only having one working ear, I don't have very good balance and a thing for heights. I always think if I go up high, I am unsafe and will die. And yet, the thought of flying in a plane or helicopter always get me excited.

The way I remember it, I could speak from birth and have never known otherwise. But according to my mother, although I *could* speak by the time I went to school, it was nowhere near as well as I can now.

Once I hit my eighth birthday, I went on to Dawn House School, up in Rainworth in Nottinghamshire.

Dawn House School: Finding a voice

*… Dawn House School is a specialist school for children
and young people aged 5-19 years with severe or complex
communication difficulty or Asperger's Syndrome. It has been
rated by Ofsted, the UK watchdog for education, as 'Outstanding'.*

I started at Dawn House School at the age of 8 years old in 1982.
With me living in Bedfordshire, I had to be a boarder at the school,
which meant that I could go home every other week. More about my
school years is coming up in the next section. I started getting a voice
when I attended the school as my day consisted of normal curriculum
and speech therapy (which usually lasted for about 2 hours, although
I could be wrong as I don't remember the *exact* length of time). The
speech therapy was intense, and we learnt the shapes and sounds of
the words and then advanced that into the form of reading. We had
to read stories out loud to the speech therapist and then answered
questions on the stories. One example that I can remember is, one of
the books that I had to read was a short story about a spy, and one
of the questions asked how I knew one of the people was a 'baddie'.
It turned out that the bad guy was wearing mirrored glasses and that
was meant to show that he was a bad guy, as you can't see the eyes. I
was baffled by that and kept on asking the speech therapist, who was
called Mrs Culloden, why that was.

I continued the speech and language therapy all the way up to
when I left school at the age of 16. As the years went on, I got better
at being able to talk and communicate with other people, although
there were times when the way people said things confused me.

We also learnt the use of money and living on our own. We had
a lesson where we had to go and live in a bungalow for a week and
fend for ourselves and then at the end of it, tell the tutor what we had
learnt. We did the normal lessons throughout the week but returned
to the bungalow at the end of the day. The lesson was called *Independent Living*, and we did this subject in the penultimate year of school.

In this subject, I think that I did quite well at it. I did manage
to look after myself along with the other student, and yet, I think

the point when I did manage to look after myself is when I went to University. But, for this subject at school, I managed. My friends probably did better than me at it than I did, but there were some who weren't as badly DLD as I was. It was quite a learning curve though, and for that, I am grateful for the school to give it to me.

Ahh, the school years...the time where you work hard and enjoy the time you had with your friends. Well, yes, it is true to me, although, at the time, I didn't enjoy it because the school was nearly 100 miles away from home.

The school was a small school, consisting of two blocks where the classrooms were, the "H Block", for accommodation (which was for the senior boys and girls. It was also in the shape of an 'H', and at the time, there was an Australian soap called 'Cell Block H', and we named it after that show, and now, they've named it as something as lame as The Flannigan's, or The Tulips...I can't remember what they've named it as), and six other units, which were also accommodation. When I first arrived, it had one block and then was extended in about 1984. We had self-contained units where weekly, and fortnightly borders stayed, who were looked after by 'house-mums' (later they came to be known as 'house-parents'), who were employees of the school and got the students up, washed, breakfasted and sent off to their lessons.

Every weekday, we would be in the classrooms from nine o'clock to half-past three, having a variety of different lessons, and then in the evening it would be either going out to the local swimming pool, watching TV or socialising with friends. At weekends, we would go out on day trips to somewhere, like Nottingham, for example, we'd go to see the Goose Fair[2]. This is the UK's largest Fair and happens every year in the summer. They'd have the usual Fairground rides, as well as exhibits. We usually go onto the dodgem cars and spend an hour on them. One time we went to it, I was on the dodgem cars with a friend, and there was a 'pile-up', and this was the point that I realised that dodgem cars had a reverse on it. I looked at my friend and said, 'Come on, let's get out of here' and just put the car into reverse. It was such a great time going to the Fair.

The number of students at the school was far less than at mainstream schools. We had 100 pupils, with about 15 pupils in each class. We studied Religious Education, Physical Education, Cooking, and more. At the time of me being there, the school didn't enter any student into exams such as GCSE's and A-Levels. Now, the school has a Further Education department at the West Notts. College and all students must take the standard GCSE and A-Levels exams.

The school years were uneventful, and when I was at school, I didn't enjoy it, but looking back at my time at the school, I look at it with fondness.

I am unable to remember much about my school years due to the disability blocking out what I did. But I am starting to remember patches of it.

What was my favourite part of school life? I would say when a tutor, called Mr Holmes, took all of us to the Peak District to do a bit of scrambling (not the professional kind, but just roaming over fallen rocks). Every weekend that he was on, he gave a choice of what we would like to do, and most of the time, it was that.

When I first joined, the school's leaving age was 13, and it changed shortly after I arrived at the school. My parents use to have a taxi taking a fellow student and me back, and I cried every time I went back to school after a weekend home. One day the parents were told that the taxi couldn't take the other student (who was from Bedfordshire as well) and I, as one time I had told the other student that the taxi wasn't taking us back to the school, they were kidnapping us. Surprise, surprise, the other boy burst into tears, and it made the taxi firm stop taking us. Our parents had to start the job of taking us up.

I think that it was also during this time when I found out what fire was. My parents had a garage and connected to it, was a 'shed' which was an extension of the garage. My parents kept a lot of wood in it (I don't remember why) but I found the matches and started using them on the wood. As you can guess, the wood went up like a tinderbox as it was dry and old. I tried to put it out with a spade, but that only fanned the fire. So, I left it. My dad saw the smoke when I was back in the house and was not happy – in fact, let us say that he was extremely angry – and put it out with water. I think he was swearing while doing it saying something like 'I wish that fucking kid would go back to school!' My Mother was also angry, and I got a serious telling off for it. I think I also got a serious beating for it. I never did it again.

I was never a very sporty person, and we had PE, which I found a cumbersome and very boring subject, but we had to do it. What was worse, I had (and still have) a fear of heights. We had in our school hall, climbing frames which went from floor to ceiling and we had to prove to the tutor, who was usually Mr Holmes, that we could do it. I got about a quarter way up, and just froze and panicked and came down. Mr Holmes (being the tutor that everyone in the school adored) started to climb up with me each week until I got to the top of the climbing frame. I felt as if I was going to be sick each week, and I took a step closer to the top.

Another thing that I didn't like in my school years was – maths! Maths was my worst enemy as I had dyscalculia (the dictionary for this says: "*severe difficulty in making arithmetical calculations, because of brain disorder*") and I remember one time when I had to do a Maths test, and I took one look at it and then said to the tutor that I couldn't do it. He replied, 'Try the best you can do it as you need to do it.' I looked at it again and then burst into tears as it terrified me. I still had to do it, and once again, I didn't get many of the answers right. My maths is a bit better today, but still not great. More on that later in the book.

By the time I was doing this maths test, I had found my voice and was using quite a lot, but I still had DLD. So, in the next part, I talk about what DLD is and how it affects me.

Every year, the school would put on a Christmas play, a play that is done by the students of the school and directed by one of the tutors. When I was at school, I remember only one of the plays – a play about Robin Hood and his merry men. It was well received by the parents, and it was said that it was the best play ever. I was Friar Tuck, and we had a student whose name is called Wayne as Robin Hood, and someone called Gary as Robin's Mother. To make me look like 'Friar Tuck', I had a cushion strapped to my stomach and had a brown overall (I don't know what you call the clothing that Friars wear) and I had the great plan of getting the 'designer' who was one of the tutors to give me a hood – unfortunately, I missed out the words 'So it hides my face'.

Robin was in green tights and the usual green clothing that every picture shows Robin as. His mother was dressed in a (what I'd call) Widow Twanky outfit!

Right, as far as my memory recalls, the story went like this. Maid Marion (who I also think was played by a guy) was kidnapped by the evil and dastardly King John and Robin Hood and his Merry men, went out to save her and also get the money that King John took from the poor. His mother joined in with the adventure and was always telling him off, like that he needs to be back in time for supper! In the end, the band of brothers managed to save Maid Marion and reclaim the money that was stolen from the poor and Robin's Mother was able to get her large TV. Yes, at every point of the adventure, she was saying that when the money was reclaimed, she'd buy a large television!

That was the gist of the play, and I'm sorry for not remembering it properly if anyone from my school is reading this book.

Anyway, after that, we didn't do any more plays as good as that I feel that it was because some of the tutors didn't have the heart to do any more plays or if people only remembered that one and it ended up being the best. I loved acting when I did this, and I wonder where I'd be now if I continued into the world of acting? I don't think I'd gone far with me being disabled and if I did, it would only be for parts that required a disabled person to be in a 'supporting role'. No big parts, like Terminator, or John Wick I don't think. Who knows, but as I'm not in that world, I can't stew over 'what ifs' can I?

As I said in the *Acknowledgements* to my house parent, Marion, I was a little trouble maker. I didn't mean to be, but it was and still is, my personality. I find being a trouble maker, as long it's for a good reason like making people laugh, is good for the soul. I was getting told off along with a fellow student by Marion, and during the telling off, she mentioned the words '…talking to you two is like banging my head against a brick wall…'. Up to this point, I was being serious and was accepting my fate, but this sent my mind into a whirl of pure wickedness. I turned around to the brick wall and said something along the lines of 'Oh, you mean like this?' and went about banging my own head against the wall. It made my fellow student laugh and made Marion even more annoyed. I think she walked off. I wouldn't recommend banging your head against a brick wall especially if it is just a straight brick wall as hurts and it knocked some of my senses out of me! The day after, I was called into a tutor's office called Mr Ludlow, who wasn't happy that I did that to Marion and it made me think that if no-one else knew about it, how did he know? It turned out that the two of them were dating, and to this day, they're still together! But anyway, I think that Marion laughs about it now when I mention it.

Out of all the house parents that I had, Marion was my favourite. She seemed to understand what the disability meant and how we were all different. I don't think there was a house parent who could compete in my eyes to Marion. As far as I can remember, it seemed that she never took a day off and she wasn't a drill sergeant unlike a previous house parent named Howard. I couldn't stand him, and it felt that if I did anything that should have made him happy, he wanted me dead. Every day we were at each other throats. On my part, I was only nice, and he mocked me for it, e.g. I'd say good morning to him when I saw him, and he mocked me the way I said it. I don't know why he hated me so much, as I saw him with other students, and he got on well with them, but I was the butt of all his jokes and bullying.

Fortunately, I have become a better person in my life, and he isn't in my memory much. But, Marion, she is.

I hadn't spoken about my other favourite at this school much, except that he took us to the Peak District and helped me over the climbing wall bars when I froze. Yup, you've guessed it – my tutor, Mr Holmes.

Mr Holmes was a wise and very knowledgeable tutor – as wise as Arthur Conan Doyle's famous detective – Mr Sherlock Holmes of 221b Baker Street, London. My tutor, Mr Holmes, was an old gent with white hair and a muscly build (more toned than Arnie build) and spoke in a soft voice. He was an old-style tutor, but fair. If you were late, you were asked why you were late, but then heard no more of it when you explained. But if you did something wrong, such as barricading yourself into a room in protest of a certain Head House Parent, you knew that he was not happy and that you shouldn't have done it. You basically received the silent treatment throughout the day and then was in detention at the end of the day where you wrote twenty thousand lines.

Despite this, Mr Holmes was a fair and a person who you knew where you stood with him. This was a guy who you could buy drinks from him and stayed in his flat chatting with him until bedtime where he shoved you off back to the 'H' Block. And, yes, it may be a bit dodgy in today's world, but this was the 80s, and I can say that nothing went on, which was dodgy. We were in a safe environment where everyone cared that we did well in our futures and get the quality of teachings that we should.

Every Christmas, we would get a Christmas card from Mr Holmes where he would sign it off with a drawing of his namesake – Sherlock Holmes. He was an amazing tutor, and I feel that if I didn't have him teaching me, I wouldn't have the enjoyment of what I see in this world. For example, I was taught about the Romans and their armies, and now, every time I have the opportunity to visit somewhere that has the Roman ruins, or the Roman clothing, I am enchanted by it. He taught us History, and it made me love history now, although not enough to become a historian, but enough to make me visit museums to see the history and to learn about WWII.

What is DLD?

In this part, I am going to talk about what DLD is. I will show you how it affects me and includes… some reports from psychologists. If you would like to skip this part and read all about me, please go to the next chapter on page 67. If you would like to know more about the disability, please continue reading.

Dysphasia is a term that was used by Afasic[3] back when I started spreading awareness of this disability in the early 1990s. The term dysphasia can be confusing because it is used to talk about language problems caused later in life by neurological conditions like stroke. In DLD, the problems aren't caused by a neurological disease but are present from birth. Afasic supports more than 6,000 children and adults across the UK who developed DLD in early life, or even in the womb. This is what has happened to me.

Although I can speak as well as the next person, albeit slow and at times hesitant, there are people with language disorders who are much worse off than me. They are not able to speak, despite them having speech therapy virtually their whole lives. They may have other disabilities that hinder them from speaking, such as cerebral palsy or dyspraxia. They may use techniques and technologies that can help them to speak. DLD is used to talk about language problems in people who don't have medical conditions like these. So DLD is rather a mystery since it doesn't have an obvious cause.

Living with DLD, in my view, is no different from living as a 'normal' person. You can still do the same things as everyone else, just with slight differences in communication. Over the years, I have had a lot of speech and language therapy at Dawn House School, which has enabled me to speak, albeit slowly, as well as everyone else. I do have some problems understanding, but if people take time, then I'm able to make myself clear for them.

DLD is not an uncommon disability. As previously mentioned, more than 6,000 children in the UK are diagnosed with DLD. However, like a fingerprint, you won't find two DLD cases who are the same. I have friends from school who are DLD but show completely different characteristics to me.

One thing I find difficult is meeting new people. I often stutter over words with 'sh' sounds. That can knock my confidence, which can make it hard to make new friends. Often, people have never heard of the disability, and don't take the time to understand. Seeing as my speech is slow, people may interrupt me or finish my sentences, which can be frustrating. I may be struggling, but I would rather people let me take my time.

I wrote a story on Facebook, about my problems meeting new people, titled "Random Thoughts: Life of a dysphasic". I have updated it for the book as it was written while I was at University. I have included it here:

"You meet someone and start chatting to them; they look at you strangely as if to say, 'Wtf you're saying?' And you realise that your words are coming out all mixed up. You try to slow your brain

out, but a whole paragraph has been sent.

"You feel the sweat start to form. You look about yourself wishing that you weren't in this situation.

"You try again, but all that comes out is stuttering. The sweat starts to form beads across your forehead and you panic even more. Hell has just come up and said 'Yup, you're in my environment now'. The guy looks at you and starts to laugh. Omg, he has laughed at you. You panic even more as another thought passes through your mind.

"You look at him, again still trying to slow your brain down so you can talk more smoothly and make sense of what this is all about. The guy has now brought over his friends, and they are making fun of you. The thought still in your mind. You panic, the sweat is taking its time to fall, but it's now visible. You try again. The stutter reappears as the brain is sending the paragraph to the mouth.

"You feel alone and helpless, and you wish that you could get out of the situation. Freak is passing through your mind. The guys are thinking about it. They hate you because you're disabled. Your head is spinning, and you feel as if you're in a non-ending roller coaster ride to Hell. You look around and try to make your goodbyes. But they want you to stay.

It is not easy having speech and language disability,
when children around you don't understand what it is

"*Taunting is on the mind of your attackers. You back away, but they follow. 'Why go? The party is just getting started' they laugh. You feel the tears welling up to your eyeballs. The stuttering is still on the go. You think 'Please mind, slow down' and yet, it doesn't. You still back away, hoping someone who doesn't think you're a freak will see you and save you. The Devil is behind the guys saying, 'You're mine now! Hahaha', and the sweat is now pouring down like Niagara Falls.*

"*The taunters see and laugh even more. 'You're a freak because you can't talk properly' they scream. You turn and run and find them chasing you laughing and shouting 'Why leave? We haven't finished with you freak!' You try to run away from them, but their breathing is on your neck. You run faster. And turn a corner, and they say, 'Why to leave?' You desperately search for an answer, but none comes. You back away and they follow still taunting.*

"You leave the room, hoping that they won't continue to follow, and sure enough, they do. "C'mon brain, slow down" you stutter to yourself. They hear this and start nudging each other while laughing. "Haha, he's talking to himself. Weirdo". You realised that they heard you and you walk faster; they walk faster. This stuttering doesn't stop, and the brain keeps on sending down the paragraphs. "Slow down, brain, slow down please" you say again. Everything is a complete shamble in the brain. Why did they see you? Why did they come and speak to you? What have you done wrong? Did you make them be like this? Did you cross paths with their parents in another life and wronged them to make them get their kids take revenge in their later life? Every minute you continue to try to slow the brain down, and after a long while, you manage to say something, and finally, you realise that your mind has slowed down. You stop and turn to them and you say something intelligent "If you bully someone who has a speech impairment or any kind of disability, it will only come back worse for you in your later life as you'll find that finding something will be a lot harder", and they look at you and are surprised. But you are now scared of them as you realise that they're another bunch of people who think you're a freak."

I felt that this was the best way to show how I felt when meeting new people. When my Facebook friends read the original, everyone complimented the story and asked me questions about it. I was not sure how the world would take it, but it was well-received. It was also nominated for the *Dusted* award, which can be given to students who have written an exceptional article for the University of Derby Student magazine. I was glad that it was nominated as it showed people what it is like to have DLD and meet new people.

Having DLD can be difficult as it takes me a lot longer to learn things. I have gone through later part of my life trying to learn web development, and yet it's been a very difficult process. I have managed to build my own website, but they haven't had the technology that is meant to be in them, such as JavaScript, or any of the backend technologies, because of it being a lot of hard work for me.

Unfortunately, there are kids and young adults who have DLD who end up offending. I have known students from my school who have ended up in prison, and a recent study led by Maxine Winstanley[4] found a disproportionate number of young people who come into contact with youth justice services (YJS) have DLD. Luckily, to my knowledge, I haven't come into contact with law enforcement, except through my jobs. Why are DLD young adults coming into contact with the law, though? It could be because the system doesn't understand the disability, or it could be their background or several different possibilities which is unanswered. Although, maybe it's just because young offenders, as a group, are likely to have significant language problems that have not been previously diagnosed.

In 2006 Lord Ramsbotham, the Chief Inspector of Prisons described a visit to Polmont Young Offenders Institute. The governor here said her most valuable member of staff was her speech and language therapist, as many of the young people who came to the institution lacked in necessary communication skills. They struggled to communicate with both their fellow inmates and the staff (https://www.theyworkforyou.com/lords/?id=2006-10-27b.1446.0)

Often the system fails children with speech, language and communication needs, so this means that they are unable to get help quick enough. The governor said, "Because these young people cannot communicate, either with each other or with us, and, until and unless they can, we do not know what it is that has prevented them from living useful and law-abiding lives, or how to begin helping them to do so in the future.' Lord Ramsbotham tried to get the then Home Secretary, Jack Straw, to put a Speech and Language Therapist (SLT) into every Young Offenders' Institute. His campaign continues to this day. Perhaps, if the children featured in the above study had been accurately diagnosed, and had received the necessary assistance, their situation could have been improved. After all, what with the help I received from Dawn House and Afasic, I didn't end up in a YOI!

Having a disabled child isn't easy for any parent. This my parents found out. You spend all your waking nights worrying about the child, and some unanswered questions that you have are endless. Will your child get the right schooling? Will, your child, get bullied?

Will your child gain friends? These were some of the questions that my parents sought to have answered. Fortunately, they were – did I get the right schooling? Yes, I did as I went to Dawn House School. Did I get bullied? Well, I did sort of at school, but I don't remember much. I remember getting bullied and then my memory shows me that I either stood up to him or he left, either way, it stopped. Did I gain friends? Yes, finally through University (*See Chapter 5 and 6 for more information*).

But with some disabled kids, this isn't so. Sometimes DLD is talked about as if it is a completely separate disorder, but it can come with different disabilities though sometimes it comes on its own. Research studies have found that it's not uncommon to have other problems with DLD, such as attentional difficulties or motor problems. Mine came with deafness, dyspraxia and dyscalculia.

When language problems occur with other more serious conditions, it is better to talk of 'Language Disorder', rather than DLD. For instance, language disorder can come along with *Asperger's Syndrome,* which is on the Autism Spectrum. This is a disability where a child has difficulty with using language as well as socialising. Autism Spectrum Disorder (ASD) covers a lot of ground and involves problems in using language appropriately (knowing what to say in a given situation). Sometimes people with Autism also have problems more like those in typical DLD – difficulties forming sentences or finding the right words. This would be a Language Disorder with Autism. Language Disorder is also common in people with intellectual disability, also known as global developmental delay.

When you are trying to identify DLD, you need to consider other things that might have caused language disorder – i.e., make a differential diagnosis. In the 2013 version of the Diagnostic and Statistical Manual of the American Psychiatric Association, they describe the following conditions that are distinct from DLD but might look like it:

- **Normal variations in Language**. It is important to realise that some children talk differently from others just because of regional, social, or cultural/ethnic variations of language (e.g. dialects). For instance, in some dialects it is normal to say, "Give me them apples" or "He don't want to do it". This is not language disorder: it's just how people in that community speak.

- **Hearing or other sensory impairment**. You would not diagnose DLD if the language disorder can be explained in terms of hearing loss. This is not always easy to judge. I am deaf in one ear, but this is not sufficient to explain my language problems, so the diagnosis of DLD still applies.
- **Intellectual disability**. Intellectual disability is diagnosed when there are problems that go beyond language to affect other aspects of life so that the child is not able to do everyday things independently. A child may have language disorder with intellectual disability: often this is caused by a known condition, such as Down syndrome. This would be treated as different from DLD, where the language problems aren't part of a broader problem.
- **Neurological disorders**. Language disorder can occur in association with neurological disorders, including epilepsy. There is a rare condition called acquired epileptic aphasia or Landau-Kleffner syndrome. Children with this condition start developing language normally but then lose language skills. This is known as language regression, and it usually is associated with epilepsy and can be part of an autistic disorder.

Wow, there are quite a few pointers there. All of these are important when a health professional starts to diagnose a child with a language disorder. Unfortunately, I don't think that it was around when I was getting diagnosed at the age of 3, but then again, it was pretty obvious that I had language problems as I was making sounds, just not the words. I wasn't able to convey my thoughts, feelings, and more except through undistinguished sounds.

The ability to communicate as we do is what distinguishes us from the animals. Spoken language allows us to convey information, express our feelings and relate to other people socially. From the moment we are born, we are taking in the world as well as the language. Every time that a mother talks to their baby, the language part of the brain is filing every word into its filing cabinet. Unfortunately, if the language department has not wired up properly when it was in the womb, this isn't possible.

Learning languages can be difficult in adulthood but isn't usually for a baby or child. We can see this when we look at how children learn different languages. A baby easily learns to distinguish the sounds that are important for their own language. For example, in a chapter on Speech and Language Difficulties from 2002, Dorothy Bishop pointed out that French has two different vowels that sounds like 'oo' to a speaker of English, but when put into a word, they sound different to a French-speaker and mean different things – 'rue' and 'roux'. An English-speaking adult who hasn't learned French finds it difficult to tell them apart, but a baby who hears French will grow up thinking they sound quite different. It also works the other way around. When an English person imitates a French accent, they say 'zat' instead of 'that'. French doesn't distinguish the 'z' and 'th' sounds, and if you don't learn to make the sounds differently when you are a young child, it is hard to hear it.

Also, we learn about the different intonations when we are babies. This can be difficult for a child with DLD to comprehend and learn. For a baby without DLD, it is easy. When you talk to a child, they will hear the intonations in your voice and will also learn it like with all the other words and sounds that you are making. In English, we use intonation to express emotions or to stress particular words. In some other languages, such as Chinese Mandarin, intonations actually define what the word means, for example the word 'ba' has four completely different meanings depending on whether the pitch is rising ('to uproot'), falling ('a harrow'), changing from fall to rise ('to hold') or at a level high pitch ('eight'). Completely different and I thought to learn English for me was difficult!

There is one thing where I am sure that I was tested on when the Health Professionals were trying to think if I had a speech and language disability or something else. And that is hearing loss. The Health Professionals will check on hearing because sometimes a language problem arises just because the child can't hear. But on the other hand, it is important not to dismiss a language disorder just because a child has some kind of hearing impairment. The key question is whether the hearing impairment can explain the language disorder. Fortunately, my mother was able to prove to the Health Professionals that I could hear, but only out of one ear, and so the language problems must be caused by something else. But, with my grandmother being on her side, they listened.

It was finally realised that I had what was called in today's terms, Developmental Language Disorder or DLD. I think when they initially diagnosed me, there wasn't much agreement about what to call it, so they talked of speech and language disability, and then everything else came into play, e.g., dysphasia, Speech, Language and Communication Needs (SLCN), etc.

When the Health Professional is diagnosing a child with a possible Developmental Language Disorder (DLD), it is appropriate to diagnose them if the child's language is getting left behind, but development is proceeding normally in other respects, and when there is no obvious explanatory factor for language delay (such as grossly abnormal home environment, global developmental delay, hearing loss or some kind of brain disease).

Over the years, researchers have shown that DLD is a very much a 'male-orientated' disability. It has been found that the ratio of genders (male:female) that are affected is around 3 or 4:1. Nobody knows why this is. Another risk factor for DLD is having a history of DLD within the family. Around one in every three children with DLD has a first-degree relative (brother, sister, mother or father) with DLD, compared with 3% of the general population – these figures come from Bishop's (2002) textbook chapter. In my family, I am the only one who has DLD, though one of my cousins has dyslexia and quite bad dyslexia. But no family member has DLD but me. I do wonder what my Mother would have done if I was a twin and my twin brother had DLD too. Would she still treat us the same as she did with me when I had no twin brother?

If I didn't have my speech therapist, Mary Courtman-Davis, teaching me how to speak as well as the speech therapists at Dawn House School, I don't think that I would be able to speak now, let alone write an autobiography. This is why intervention at an early age is good. Speech and language therapists (SLT) use many different methods to help children learn language. When I was learning, I was basically drilled into getting to speak. Although it worked, things have changed. Back in the day, so to speak, speech therapists used imitation and elicitation methods – they would get children to repeat back sentences, or describe pictures, trying to get them to pick up the sentence structure. One of the problems for many children with DLD is learning grammatical structures – how words go together. You can understand what a child means if they say, 'Him play there' rather than 'He is playing there', but it doesn't sound right. Most children learn quickly to speak like an adult, but for a child with DLD, it is not obvious, and they have to have a lot of help.

Like with everything, I will never know what would happen if my parents didn't fight for my corner when I was little. It comes down to the 'What if' statements. I feel that I could be worse off than I am today without speech therapy, and if my parents didn't listen, then I could have a lot more problems than I normally do. Fortunately, this didn't happen, and I am making up for the 15 years of not being able to talk and boring Libby and everyone else who knows me!

I'm sure at the time of me not being able to talk at the age of 3 years old; the professionals would say to my mother, 'Oh, don't worry Mrs Quinn, he is just a late-talker', and I'm sure that she'd argue the point that I wasn't. But it always seems if a child has DLD, it is easy for the doctor to identify the child as a 'late-talker'. However, although some children do catch up in language after a late start, that wasn't true in my case.

But seriously, when your child speaks to you, do you listen to them? Moreover, if your child is disabled, do you listen to them? As Roulstone and McLeod showed, it only takes a moment to realise why listening to children is important. A child can show you the world through their eyes, and if they are disabled, then it becomes even more important. When I was young and was unable to speak, it was all by gestures and sounds to alert my parents to what I was seeing. It was the world that I could not understand because I didn't know why people didn't understand what I was saying.

I've met people with DLD who are in jobs where I only can wish that I could be. I feel that the job which I am in at the moment is good, but I like learning new things and stretching my mind to become better in anything I want to do. I can't say that I have the ability to be an 'entrepreneur' as I feel that you have to be extremely intelligent for that, also know where you'd like to be in the job. But employers do need to promote opportunities for self-employment, entrepreneurship, the development of cooperatives, and starting one's own business for people with disabilities. I've always looked at *Virgin StartUp*[5] and wondered what I would pitch to Richard Branson about if I decided to start up my own business and approached him for help and I never could think of anything. I feel that I don't have the skills to start up my own company – not even in security. Even if I did have an idea of where to place my business, I wouldn't know where to start building it up.

I know one thing, I would make sure that I could accommodate disabilities within my company as I would have to ensure that reasonable accommodation is provided to persons with disabilities in the workplace and even if I just employed people with DLD, I'd make sure that I could accommodate for them.

Communication is not just important for work. It is a key factor in life. Even animals who don't have language still communicate. This allows them to socialise and know who is at the top of the pecking order. And for humans, communication is at the core of all social interaction. In his report in 2008, John Bercow argued that children need effective communication skills to engage with others and thrive. But without communication skills, what has the child got to learn, achieve, make friends and interact with the world they live in? Nothing. It will be a difficult and scary world if the child doesn't get any help in learning the language to communicate and at times, very lonely.

For this, life as a DLD child or young adult, we can face a significant ongoing struggle to face the ability to communicate. In the UK, the Government have been doing a lot to make the lives of disabled children, including those with DLD, better. Their flagship programme, *Every Child Matters*[6], aimed to help children and young people to be healthy and to stay healthy. But this is not easy to do. It is not easy to fix language – it needs a lot of expert help. But it is important to do this because having problems in this area puts children and young people at risk

As well as providing services to work with children, we need to create a better understanding of the general public. Children with DLD feel isolated because other children and adults of the mainstream world, don't always understand what is wrong with them. Some people think that they are lazy or even slow, but this is not the case.

It can be a long and slow process getting a diagnosis of DLD, and this is not helped by the fact that so many people have not heard of it. In the early years of a child's life, a speech and language problem is one of the most common reasons why parents consult their doctor, often leading to a referral for speech and language therapy. Often, it is not immediately obvious that the problem a child has DLD. Once the child has a proper diagnosis by a professional, they can start to get appropriate help.

A lot of research has been done trying to work out what types of underlying problems are involved in DLD. It is not simply because language is so complicated: it involves listening to sounds and hearing differences between them, linking up the sounds with meanings, putting words together in sentences, and working out how to translate thoughts into a series of movements of the mouth. So, a whole range of language and cognitive processes needs to be smoothly integrated, and a breakdown in any one process can cause problems.

Children with language impairments are usually hindered by having a short-term memory problem. This I can relate to as my memory only goes back to the age of 15, while Libby (see more of her in *Chapter 6*) can talk about her life going back to when she was small (this often makes me jealous of her, because I have only some remnants of the life before the age of 15). Afasic held a symposium in 2007, and the book of the proceedings gives more information about this (see Norbury et al. 2008). There is research that confirms that children with Language Impairments do less well with a range of short-term memory, and working memory tasks Afasic held a symposium in 20xx, and the book of the proceedings gives more information about this. There is research that confirms that children with Language Impairments do less well with a range of short-term memory and working memory tasks.

Children with communication difficulties are being left to struggle as cuts mean they miss out on vital speech and language therapy, a survey has found.

There were reports that some children were waiting up to a year to see a speech and language therapist (SLT), up from about 18 weeks three years ago. A study by the Royal College of Speech and Language Therapists found 52 per cent of SLTs reported budget cuts over the past year.

Kamini Gadhok, chief executive of the college, said that expert senior staff were being made redundant and children with speech, language and communication problems were having to wait longer for treatment or not being seen at all. "Short-sighted cuts will have a significant and avoidable impact on a whole generation of children and once these services are lost it will take years to rebuild them," she said.

Ms Gadhok warned that the Government's new development checks for two-year-olds by health visitors would fail to benefit children if there were no longer enough SLTs to support those identified as needing help.

Article from the Independent

It can be difficult to get recognition for DLD services because it is often a hidden disability – the problems are often not obvious when you first meet a child or adult with DLD. Speech and language therapists seem to have endless battles to get funding. The difficulties in children with Speech and Language Impairments (SLI) has been in the news recently. Back in 2014, the newspaper, *The Independent*, reported about the cuts which the government were creating amongst Speech and Language Therapists (SLT).

Without the speech therapy that I received while I was at school, I wouldn't be talking as well as I am in my present life. Speech therapy is much needed for all tomorrow's children who are born with Speech, Language and Communication Needs (SLCN).

Although they struggle to get funding, speech therapists are clear about what is needed. Like with most things in life, there are recommendations for delivering support for people with DLD. The Royal College of Speech and Language Therapists produced a list of recommendations. I will put a few of them here; to find more of the recommendations, see the paper that is referenced at the end:

Recommendation 1:

Any speech and language therapist (SLT) working with children should:

- Identify the speech, language, communication or eating/drinking needs of the child as part of, or regarding, the appropriate multidisciplinary team (this does not imply a static membership, more the team of relevant professionals for the individual child)
- Identify the functional impact of these needs
- Consider the most appropriate context for support, i.e. which settings are most relevant to the child and their family
- Identify the contribution of the speech and language therapist as part of the wider team working with the child to meet the child's needs – including the full range of options from advice to colleagues through setting up programmes to direct intervention where appropriate.

Recommendation 2:

Services should offer the full range of support for children, including direct intervention where appropriate while ensuring overall management includes goals relating to activity and participation, managed by those most relevant the child.

Recommendation 3:

The RCSLT regards trans-disciplinary working as central to work with children. The RCSLT supports the exploration of SLT roles within trans-disciplinary models and the development of new models that maximise the contribution of SLTs while ensuring that the specialist contribution to the system is recognised as essential. Emerging key worker roles and lead professional roles are also central to this model of working if it is to be successfully implemented for the benefit of children and their families. (Gascoigne, 2006)

If speech therapists don't make the recommended moves to accommodate a child with DLD, then it will be a difficult life for the child.

In every country, across the world, there will be children who have DLD, though the terminology and available support varies widely from one country to another. There is a general recognition that all agencies working with children have a key role to play in all aspects of the child's development for them to achieve the five outcomes to:

1   Be healthy
2   Stay safe
3   Enjoy and achieve
4   Make a positive contribution
5   Achieve economic well-being

The child will be able to work with the SLT and develop their speech and language. Even if the parents have to get the child up at 06:00 every morning and bribe the child with chocolate drops like mine did, before making a trip to see the SLT!

Throughout the school life of the child, and possibly the future, the authorities, like teachers, need to put in place special help to allow the child to get through life to the point that they want to be. If this means that the kid is mentored, one-to-one, every day, it will help the child and the tutors to learn about each other. Not every DLD child will learn fast, and those who do are the lucky ones. Even at home, the journey to adulthood also needs help from the parents guiding the child onto the path of their choice by giving them every chance to succeed in life.

A report was commissioned and published in 2018 as the government's response to the Bercow review of services for children and young people with speech, language and communication needs. It recommended that we needed better delivery to achieve better outcomes for children and young people. This report was aiming to help parents and professionals to find the most useful ways of helping children to reach their communication potential.

With me, it was for people to take time out to listen to me and be patient with me. The endless hours of speech therapy that my cohorts and I received at school also helped. A child with DLD may need teaching that is different to the other members of the class. It can help if the tutor develops a routine for the student to assist them through their education life; whether it is 1-to-1 mentoring or a classroom assistant, the help should be there for the child.

As I mentioned earlier, we don't just need more services for children, and we also need more people knowing about DLD. The response to the Bercow Report (Bercow: Ten Years On) gives information about the Communication Trust (founded by British Telecom), Afasic, and ICAN and the Council for Disabled Children, who help raise awareness of the importance of speech, language and communication among people working with children. These organisations also enable practitioners to access the best training and expertise to support all children's communication needs. The Communication Trust hosts the 'what works' website[7], which adds to what Afasic has on their website – their link is at the end of the book.

Afasic offered key financial support to another small campaign, set up by a group of academics and a speech-language therapist, called *Raising Awareness of Language Learning Impairment (RALLI)* now known as *Raising Awareness of Developmental Language Disorder (RADLD)*. As the title says, it's trying to raise public awareness of Developmental Language Disorder, mainly through YouTube information videos, and it has been supported by the Communication Trust and ICAN as well. I have been on the Advisory Board for about three years now and went and involved myself with the meetings about DLD and SLI.

Afasic has also played a key role in supporting parents. I'm sure that my parents, and every parent across the globe, looked forward to the first landmark of the child being able to speak, but like with me, in some cases, that isn't to be. Of course, babies can communicate before they start to speak. They use noises and gestures and facial expressions to get their meaning across. But once they get words, it makes a big difference. I think my parents would have been worried to the ends of the earth, if it was not for the rock in the lives, as in my grandmother. It can't be easy to see your child reach two years old and realise that your baby isn't saying its first words. Think about it; there are many reasons why a child may not produce their first spoken words, but it will always be a source of worry. Delays or differences in early words usually indicate there is a problem. It could mean the child has a hearing impairment, general learning disabilities or autism. I think that when I was younger, my mother took me to get my IQ test done, and it was between 110 and 120, but I am not at all sure about it. Over the years, the only area of the brain which was not functioning well was the language side. I have difficulties with language, i.e. producing words to communicate and/or understanding what is said to them, while "everything else" appears to be normal.

Fortunately, I have 'everything else' to be as normal as it can be. I still am deaf in the left ear and have other disabilities such as the ones that have been said already. I wasn't any different to anyone else until I opened my mouth and stuttered out my words to another person. I then was spotted at 'not being normal' by some people and in some cases was treated like a freak. Because affected children look like their typically developing peers, DLD is a hidden disability.

Given the importance of language to human behaviour, it is not surprising to find that language difficulty is a risk factor for associated difficulties in other aspects of children's lives. When I meet someone new, or even talking on the phone, I find it a massive and sometimes embarrassing struggle to talk or interact with them. That's why I was delighted when I got the texting technology from my mobile company at the time. It used to take me a week or more to open myself up to people as I was terrified that they'd tease me for having DLD. In some children's lives, with DLD, they could find it effortful to learn to talk, and these difficulties can be persistent.

As an adult and a Vice President for a National Charity, I have found through my work that the disability is not just hidden from sight, but a very neglected disability – something emphasised by the RADLD campaign. If you watch the News, you'll see information about other disabilities, such as autism, dyslexia, and so on, but not for DLD. This can be seen in the number of grants and funding that goes to the other disabilities compared to what DLD gets. In 2010, Dorothy Bishop did an analysis of research publications and grants that confirmed this impression, showing that DLD attracted far less research funding and led to fewer publications than many other conditions that were similar in terms of how common they were and how much impact they had. Perhaps the most striking comparison was with attention deficit hyperactivity disorder (ADHD). DLD is as common as ADHD and clinicians rated DLD and ADHD as similar in terms of the impact they had on a person's life. Between 1985-2009, there were 1,140 publications on DLD in Web of Science, compared to 12,631 on ADHD. Between 2008 and 2009, funding was 19 times greater for ADHD than for DLD. This seems completely wrong, as it should be equal. I think that DLD is as important as any other disabilities in the world. Yes, I know that I would say it because I have it, but listen, I feel that DLD should have as much right to be noticed as other conditions. Children are being born who have it due to neurodevelopmental problems before they are born. And what life will they have if no-one recognises a disability that can begin in the womb?

Remember me comparing the disability to a fingerprint? If you think I'm making it up, trust me, I'm not. DLD is a hidden disability. Most individuals with DLD can talk, and their difficulties are not always obvious, but each person with DLD is different in terms of strengths and weaknesses.

One way in which children vary is in terms of control of movements, so-called motor skills, e.g. when you go and pick up a drink; you use your hand to reach out and grab the drink and then take it to your mouth. When I was younger, my motor skills weren't as good as they are now. Well, this isn't the best of my abilities, and if you ever saw me doing the breaststroke, you will know what I mean! I look like an animal drowning when I have to do the breaststroke leg kick!

Also, having a poor ability in the motor skills region, some children, like me, are not good at the gesture, which involves complex integration of social, cognitive and motor skills. So, growing up, I had to learn a whole new set of skills which other children found easy to do. It continued to be difficult when I had to find that with emotions and to speak; you needed also know the millions of facial expressions that accompanied it, e.g. expressions for *sad, angry, disappointed, surprised, elated,* etc.

Another problem I have is dyscalculia, which is a disability that hits the maths portion of the brain. This disability I had throughout my life, and still, have got although not as bad as when I was younger. But with many kids and young adults, such difficulties present a barrier to learning in the classroom at school, getting a job, and being financially independent. I have certainly witnessed the latter as I'm always broke! It can be a massive pain. So, with this disability, it is harder for me to look after my financial affairs, although, I am a lot better than before.

I feel that if I had the right tuition at school, I might have been able to combat dyscalculia to a certain extent. Nowadays, there is a lot more accessible equipment for children and young adults to get the help that they need. Because typical developing children are faster at learning than their peers who have dyscalculia there is a widening gap in the learning. I can also see this as I have seen my mainstream peers going into high-flying jobs, and I'm in a low paid job and having trouble finding new jobs because I don't have the right qualifications. I would rather be in that high-paid job, but I find it hard studying for those jobs.

Although it is getting better now, or I'm managing to cope with it, I still have the disability that I call 'dyscalculia' which is also known as 'the maths disability'. If you give me a sum, for example, $20038 \div 108$ (which is a 'long division sum with a remainder') I have no clue how to complete it. I understand it can be easy for some people. When it comes to money, I am equally stuck. I try my best, but it sometimes is not easy. In a recent report, it has been found that 80% of young adults with DLD have trouble with finances, compared to 92% of aged-match peers. I know people who have DLD who have got financial help from outside sources, but I have had help from family members, especially from my mother. Fortunately, now I do manage my own finances, not very well, but I can cope. I still have trouble seeing when I should stop spending, but I think that comes with learning and realising that I need to look at my bank account more often. If I was wealthy, this wouldn't happen!

Along with having DLD, I had to learn all the different names for it. When I found out that I had a disability, it was only called speech and language handicapped; then, as I got older, I found other names for it. Once, I hit college; I kept on hearing DLD hence why it's the title of this book! But, having so many names for one disability, can lead to confusion and it also holds back research on DLD. In a survey reported by Dorothy Bishop in 2014, she found there were 132 different terms, with 33 that had 600 or more returns on Google Scholar. So, you can understand why that is a massive problem for the researchers who are trying to study the disability.

In this book alone, I've probably used several different names for my disability, e.g. *dysphasia, SLI, SLCN, DLD,* and maybe more. The last three abbreviations are Specific Language Impairments (SLI), Speech, Language and Communication Needs (SLCN), Developmental Language Disorder (DLD). Even for me, it does get a tad confusing. I prefer dysphasia, but I know that it's not accepted amongst the speech and language therapists at the Royal College of Speech Therapy (RCST) and Afasic hasn't used it since the 90s. But I find it easier to say, than the others!

People who are working in the sciences that deals with communications and disorders have noted that unfortunately, there is a lack of terminology that is consistent with the disability. Fortunately, they agree that there must be a specific terminology that is used time after time that is required to help communication with:

- Families,
- Individuals
- Professionals across the Health and Education sectors and all disciplines concerned with language problems
- The media
- Policymakers and service planners; and
- The research community(s) (Reilly, Bishop, & Tomblin, 2014)

to better understand what causes the problem or problems. This will determine the commonness and, importantly, what are the best way of delivering the most effective help for the child with communications problems.

So, with all these names, it is a wonder if anyone can say what the disability is. For children and young people with language problems and their families, the professionals can never agree on either 'what it is' and 'what it is called', but they know that it is critical. Unfortunately, there is still a long way to go before we can agree the subject of 'what it is' and 'what it is not', but we have at least now had a study to try and get consensus, and it has agreed on the term DLD. This will help with research in finding how to help children and young people with DLD.

As previously mentioned, DLD was the term agreed upon by a group of experts who took part in a discussion process in a project called CATALISE. I have used several synonyms for the disability, but fortunately, the term Developmental language disorder (DLD) was the term agreed by a panel of 57 experts. Why is this? Well, people who worked with children and young adults who have the disability wanted just one word for the disability. I can't see why this could be a problem, considering you have one word for 'Autistic', 'dyslexia', etc. The label would avoid problems that may arise if you had other words for DLD. It could co-occur with milder neurodevelopmental disorders where there was no other medical condition. I still like the label 'dysphasia', only because the others are a bit of a mouthful for someone like me. From all the surveys that was done, the recommendation that the term 'specific language impairment' (SLI) be abandoned in favour of 'developmental language disorder' (DLD). I definitely agree with this as it is a mouthful, and I'm not very good at saying 'specific'.

Anyway, I think that's enough psychology of the disability, so why don't we go back to talking about my life...

CHAPTER 2

Mid-teens

When a man is asked to make a speech,
the first thing he has to decide is what to say.

—Gerald R. Ford

SO, MY LIFE MOVES TO WHEN I'M 16 YEARS OLD, IN 1990. I have left school and am heading off to college. The college is *Dunstable College of Further Education*, now known as *Central Bedfordshire College*. I was put into a Special Needs class. This was okay for a year, as I was at the top of the class. After about a year, I got bored and asked (with my Mother help, which turned out to be good as I found out later because the support tutors feared her) the college to get me into the mainstream classes. Which, they were more than helpful. During my time in the Special Need's class, I had boring lessons, for example, we learnt how to 'clean windows' and had to clean some of the college's doors windows. I found that this wasn't stretching my mind but kept at it in the hope that it would change. We had other lessons, but I don't remember the lessons.

I moved into English for two years, where I learnt about Shakespeare. We had to listen to the Mark Antony speech, where the first lines were:

"Friends, Romans, countrymen, lend me your ears;
"I come to bury Caesar, not to praise him."

And I remember that I was so bowled over by the speech that it made me love *Julius Caesar* so much that I went home and instantly told my Mother when she returned from work. We sat with each other for a few hours and discussing why Mark Antony gave the speech. I have always loved Shakespeare from an early age. My Mother arranged a theatre trip for me on my birthday when I was about 7-8 years old to go and see '*The Comedy of Errors*' with my cousins, my aunt, herself and my father and we were given the Directors' Box and she said that she remembered 'two 7 or 8-year-olds just howling over the play' and then going back to my grandmother's and reacting the door letterbox scene and my grandmother being appalled at it!

I remember another point now, where my aunt (my Mother's sister), was staying with us for a while as I think my Mother was in hospital and we were in the kitchen, and I was reading out poems, like *The Tyger* by William Blake and she was explaining how I should read it, what it was about and more. My aunt was an English Tutor by training and taught at one of the London schools. It was an interesting time in my life.

But I digress. In about 1993, I went on to do the *BTEC Diploma in IT Applications*. Now, BTEC was completely different from how they are now. In the BTEC that I did, I think that we didn't do any exams, it was all based on coursework. We did multiple subjects in the course, such as programming (using Pascal) and a lot of essay-based subjects. I can't remember what I did in the course, due it being a long time ago from the time of writing this autobiography. In this course, I found that the tutors were very helpful, and they helped me in passing the course.

When I was on the BTEC course, I managed to meet two people who were classmates of mine, named Paul and Philip. We became good friends, and to this day we still chat so often. Paul was an ex-amateur boxer and trained in weights, and Philip was a sci-fi nerd who adored *Star Trek*® and had cerebral palsy. Both were very good at computing and went on to work in Computing after the course.

I have asked Phil to write a bit about how we met, and this is his bit for the autobiography:

"When I think of Damian "Damo" Quinn I think to how he was when I first met him at Dunstable College; shy, quiet and didn't talk to many other students on our course. Now how he had grown into someone who I am proud to call a friend and is confident in different situations that, when I first met him, he would have run in the other direction to take himself away from dealing with things.

"I first met Damo when we were both at Dunstable College studying I.T Applications. Damo was very quiet, and I was also, due to being out of my comfort zone. We started talking one day and found that we seemed to get on. When we started talking Damo was very quiet and slow in replying and would get muddled saying things, being disabled myself, I grew to accept this and tried to build Damo's confidence in speaking and asking for things. Our friendship became so strong that most of the time, I knew what he was going to say. I remember while at college together we used to enjoy going to Dunstable Downs in our free periods, picking up food and drink along the way. We used to go into shops and ask for things. Damo was very hesitant in asking, and I started to ask on his behalf, but that soon changed. I used to say to him, "I am here if you need help, but you need to ask", on occasions people in shops looked at me for help, but I used to say, "He is your customer he's the one with the money, if he needs my help he'll ask me". Saying that to people in shops probably wasn't the best way of dealing with his questions but looking back Damo learnt that I was there to help if he needed it.

"My friendship with Damo was so strong that a lot of people used to say we were two peas in a pod, wherever one of us was at college,

the other wasn't far behind. We used to spend a lot of time in "The Centre" in Milton Keynes or London "window shopping", spending time doing what friends do when they get on so well. One thing that Damo introduced to me was going to the theatre to watch shows. This is something I'm happy that we did because he showed me that shows are fun and broadened my cultural awareness; this is something that I had never thought of doing before.

"I have learnt a lot from Damo, and as the years have moved on and our friendship has grown, I am so happy that he has found himself a lovely lady who loves him. He has grown into someone who isn't scared of putting his thoughts, views and feelings out there into his everyday life and will talk to anybody who he meets."

I want to thank Phil for doing that.

The year is 1997, and I leave Dunstable College and move onto another college, which was coincidentally near my school, called Portland College for the Registered Disabled[8] where I did City and Guilds Support Users of I.T. For this course, I gained a 'Credit'. This course was quite a good course where I learnt how to support users of I.T. Although I gained a credit for the course, it taught me how to use software such as Microsoft Office 97 which contained Word, which was a word processing software, Excel, which was a spreadsheet software, Access, which was a database and PowerPoint which was a presentation software, for me to support someone who was having difficulty with it. I also learnt to use an accounting package which was Sage, which was quite interesting to learn as I had never used an accounting package before then.

At Portland College, I met some amazing people who just 'got up and said yes I can do this' and didn't let the disability stop them from enjoying life. With the people who I kept in touch with, mainly through Facebook, have gone on to do very good jobs. No-one at the college thinks themselves different to anyone else; we were all in the same boat.

Between me being at Dunstable College and going to Portland College, my Mother gave me an idea of going on the Tall Ships[9] and I said yes. So, I went on a short sail which was from their port, Southampton to Liverpool via Dublin. We picked up a Tall Ship race from Dublin to Liverpool, and when I came into the dock, I loved it so much, I managed to persuade Mother to let me go back on. So, a week later, I was back on it, going from Gran Canaries to Southampton. Unfortunately, I didn't get as far as Southampton because I had to get off in the Azores due to having a fit. Fortunately, I haven't ever had a fit since being on the ships. During the time, I was on the ship; I had to scrub the decks, deal with the sails, and keep watch. I didn't go up the mast except in the Gran Canaries with two of the crewmen helping me, due to my fear of heights, and when I did, that was a big deal for me, and I thought that I had achieved something. Unfortunately, I am still terrified of heights.

Ahh, the feel of weightlessness with nothing to hurt you…well, maybe a few rocks, coral, and odd fish who's a bit hungry. Yes, you may have guessed it, I became a diver.

I joined *Chiltern Divers* in Leighton Buzzard and started my long journey to become a diver.

Work Experience

From Portland College, I had work experience at *Argos Head Office* in Milton Keynes. At Argos, I was supporting users of I.T., as I did at the College. We had a job board where we would look to see what is needed to be done, and we would go off and deal with it. As I couldn't drive, I only dealt with the jobs which were in the Milton Keynes Head Office. I also learnt how to put a computer together from scratch, as I was asked to help an employee who was doing the job. I found that I was enjoying it and wanted to know more about it. But the placement came to an end and unfortunately as apparently "there were no jobs" for me to have a permanent job. So, I left.

After this, I was trying to find a job in Computing but was unsuccessful. I found that my qualifications weren't what the companies were looking for. I went on to do an Office qualification through a *'Learning shop'* (which is a learning environment where people who were not in a job could go and build up some skills that will get them back into work. Unfortunately, I don't think they're about anymore), and ended up teaching the students who were having problems. Through the company, I was put on work experience to do Support of I.T. at *Gedas* in Milton Keynes. *Gedas* instead put me onto the Web Development team, and I found another area of I.T. which I enjoyed. Here I learnt how to create a website by using Dreamweaver™. I also learnt about using Flash™ and Fireworks™. These products at the time of me being at Gedas was created by Macromedia®, which was then taken over by Adobe®. I built a website to go onto the Intranet that explained what DLD was. Look, even then, I was spreading awareness! Though, as I have improved to build the websites, I have realised that it wasn't the best that I've done. More on that later.

Following Gedas, I went on to do NVQ in Computer Maintenance, Networking and Web Mastering (like website design) at a local college in Luton called *Barnfield Technology Centre*. I did work experience here at *Luton University* (now known as *University of Bedfordshire*) doing web development.

While doing the course, I learnt how to put a computer together from scratch, which I found quite easy to do and even went as far as building a computer myself. I also learnt how to network a room, and I didn't quite enjoy that as it was very fiddly and having dyspraxia that was not an easy job to do. Although I am not sure why I was okay with building a computer, I had problems with networking. Maybe it was because the cables and wires were a lot smaller than the insides of the computer. Anyway, I also learnt how to design a website. Although it wasn't very well designed because I had just really started learning web design and wasn't quite use to it, I did use it to spread awareness of the disability. Although, the site didn't go up onto the Internet, or at least I think it didn't.

Life After College

After I had completed college, I continued to try to get a job in I.T. but unsuccessful. The qualifications were wrong type as companies were looking for qualifications such as professional or University qualifications. While I have been doing these qualifications at college,

my disability was a hit or miss kind of situation as I had some difficulty with some people, but mostly no difficulty.

While I was at Dunstable College, I used Dunstable Leisure Centre to get fitter and build up muscle and met someone who helped me
to do the weights, who was called Andrew, aka Panda (don't ask me
why he was called *Panda* as I don't remember).

While I was at college, I use to swim for my local swimming club,
Linslade Crusaders[10]. Yeah, I was part of a swimming club. Here, I
managed to get better at swimming, not perfect, but better than I was
before attending the club. I also did the galas, and all I had cheering
was the other participants from the club, my family never joined me
to cheer me on although, my Mother did attend once and even at that
point, she didn't cheer me on, and I think she wasn't even interested
in seeing me doing the swimming. I think quite a few things that I
did, she just put it down to a 'phase', and at times, she said 'Don't do
such and such as it's not real' even though I was good at whatever she
was talking about. For example, we went to America to visit my Dad's
family and friends, and after a while, I slipped into the accent as you
would when you were a child. After we got back, we went out the
following summer, and before we went, I was told by my Mother to
not speak in the accent as 'it was not real, and it could offend people
in the country'. We arrived at the friends' house, and the kids asked
why I wasn't talking to them in the accent as it was very good. I told
them that I wasn't allowed. I have never been able to slip back into
the accent properly ever again. Anyway, I digress, once I found that I
couldn't get a job in I.T., I decided to get a job as a lifeguard at *Tiddenfoot Leisure Centre*[11] in Leighton Buzzard. I approached the Operations Manager, who was Panda, and asked him if I could have a job
as a lifeguard. He put me on the *National Pool Lifeguard Qualification
(NPLQ)* course which I passed with flying colours.

Yet, I didn't find a problem with lifeguarding, and only found one
fellow lifeguard who called me 'slow' when I was trying to get a kid
out of the lanes when it was a public swim (the lanes were for people
aged for 16+ and he was about 11-12 years old). I didn't like the lifeguard after that day. But anyhow, if I did have a problem, I had a team
to back me up who were in generally okay with me. After the first

year, I became tough and was tough on the customers of the pool. For example, if I saw anyone who was doing anything that could injure themselves, I was quick to remove them from the pool. I found that it gained my respect, and the customers (especially the teens) were respecting me and wouldn't mess around. I quickly became known amongst them, and they always acknowledge me when they saw me outside work.

During this time, I decided that I wanted to join a club, and I found that I knew someone in St John Ambulance, who was a swimming teacher for Linslade Crusaders Swimming Club. I spoke to him one day while he was on duty at the town's carnival about St John Ambulance and he said that I should come along one evening to try it out, so I did.

I have found that I enjoyed it and hadn't ever left. Once again, my disability didn't hinder the post of being a St John Ambulance member. I met a lot of people through it and gained quite a lot of friends through it, and still am friends with a few of them even now.

Away from work and first aid career, I have found that some people don't like that I am disabled, but these are far and few between.

CHAPTER 3

Family life

HAVING A DISABILITY CAN MAKE FAMILY LIFE DIFFI-CULT. This can happen if one member of the family is disabled and getting special treatment, while the other siblings are cast aside. Fortunately, that didn't happen in my family.

I was born into a middle-class family. My mother, when I was born, wasn't working and shortly after, got a job as a secretary with NAMM. My father was working as an animator. I have one older half-sister. My half-sister was at school in Leighton Buzzard.

My half-sister, Andrea, was at Vandyke School, Leighton Buzzard, and was very talented in music. After Vandyke, she went to the Royal Academy of Music in London and studied conducting. After leaving the Academy, she entered a competition in 1993 called 'Conduct for Dance' and successfully won it. She was plucked up by the Royal Ballet (Covent Garden) to be their Musical Director and gained a lot of fame from patrons and the orchestra. In 1991, she got married to a doctor, and they moved to New Jersey as Andrea received a job from the New York City Ballet (2001-2006) as the Music Director. To find out more about her, she can be found on her website[12]

My mother continued through the ranks of the organisation getting to CEO of NAMM and with the company she travelled all over the country and sometimes Europe. She worked hard all the way up to until she became ill and had to retire from the company. Afterwards, she worked as a temp with *Deloitte and Touche (Deloitte)* and the *National Energy Foundation (NEF)*. Her illness took her, and she had to retire from those jobs, and in November 2013, she died in a car accident.

My father came to the UK in 1967 and married my Mother in 1972. When he came over, he was working as an animator and a few years later, worked as a photographer at *Sotheby's*, the major auction house. He worked there until his retirement. When my Mother became ill, he was looking after her and was amazing at it. He could be relied on her to do a lot of the things she asked him.

Growing Up

Growing up in a family such as this was good. I didn't understand much of what was going on, but I had the love and care from my family. At an early age, I was very talkative, and I would have the family stopping to listen to me because they wanted me to practice. One day, my Mother was on the phone to someone, and I came in and started to speak to her, and she had to say to the other person '*Just hold on one minute, Damian is trying to speak*' and then turned to me and said '*Yes, darling*' and allowed me to speak. The level of speech that I had when I was small was not good. When I wanted to call my mother, it was '*Mimmy*', and I didn't have a word for my father. Whenever my mother went to work, my father came into the room to wake me up, and I'd wake up and then scream as it wasn't my mother. He usually had to shut the door and wait until I calmed down and then get me up. There is a picture of me with his Uncle, and I was looking over the shoulder at my mother, checking that she didn't leave the room.

My mother joined a charity that wasn't all that well known at that time as it is now, called Afasic. They used to do Activity weeks where the parents would send their kids off to the holiday destination (which usually was somewhere in the United Kingdom) and have a week's break from them. I joined the holidays when I was five years old.

On the holidays, every child had one 'link' or 'helper' who would look after them and make the holiday enjoyable for them. My first holiday was in Colwyn Bay, North Wales and I enjoyed it so much, when the following summer came, I was excited to go on the holiday. Although, when I was on holiday in Colwyn Bay, I found out that I didn't like jellyfish as I got stung by one! At the age of 5, that hurts, and I screamed and cried quite a lot. Unfortunately, my link didn't see it and didn't understand what I was saying. Don't know how I knew what a jellyfish was, but just knew that it was evil, and they didn't like me!

Throughout my life, I have enjoyed quite a lot of things. I have managed to water-ski, scuba dive (I am a qualified PADI diver, although the membership may have expired as I haven't dived for ages), enjoyed the cinema, the theatre, travelling, and cooking, to name but a few. My Mother fought until her last day to give me a better life and to have a variety of experiences.

So, another thing that I enjoy is the theatre, which will I talk about further in the book, but I thought that I should put a bit here in the introduction. Like most people, I adore the theatre as it has live actors who if they forget their lines, they must continue with their part. It can't be done in another 'take' as the movies. I, and my wife Libby and her Mother, recently went to see Oscar Wilde's *Importance of Being Ernest* starring David Suchet. The play was magnificent and well worth seeing. During the play, the actors ended up corpsing quite a lot, but they managed to keep it under control. Another play or at least musical (which I also adore) that I saw was a musical about Tammy Wynette, the singer of 'Stand by Your Man' and the narrator completely forgot his lines of one part of the musical and had admitted it. He went off and came back on a few minutes later, and just continued. The audience erupted into laughter and then applauded him when he came back on. Now, I was with my Mother, and I turned to her and said, 'I never saw that happening', and she told me it happens quite a lot.

I also enjoy the movies, but it doesn't give me a similar kind of enjoyment as the Theatre, but I still like it. The genre that I enjoy is thought-provoking films, comedies and some sci-fi. With Sci-fi, I adore Star Wars, although you won't ever find me dressing up as Darth Vader to go to a Sci-fi event! I enjoy watching them. I can't understand why people would go and watch horror. Why would you want to be terrified for 2 hours of your life? I will always avoid Horror movies like the plague.

That is the trouble when you have DLD, very few people can understand you. Fortunately, with my family, they could and accepted me how I was. I guess if you have a disabled son, you should. Otherwise, it could be conceived as neglect. Having a disabled sibling isn't a problem if you love him or her for who they are. There are too many people out in the world who will put themselves through a lot of tests to get that 'ideal' child. I feel that is not right. If the child comes out as disabled, then accept it as your life will become amazing as you will see the world in a different light. You will fight their corner and fight for the right to the child having a 'normal' life.

All disabilities have their challenges, some more, some less, but my experience is with DLD. I don't know all the disabilities, but I do take an interest in others. Like my Mother, I fight for and spread awareness of those with DLD or children with speech and language impairments. It is very important for children to get the correct support, so I work to spread awareness of the ICAN schools, like Dawn House School.

More on this subject will come up in Chapters 9 and 10.

A Town Called Leighton Buzzard

Leighton Buzzard is 37.311 miles north as the crow flies from London. The town is nestled in the heart of Bedfordshire with Milton Keynes to the north, and Luton and Dunstable to the south. It is quiet, but a bustling town with its High Street full of shops and back alley coffee shops. In recent year, some of the big chain shops have come into the town.

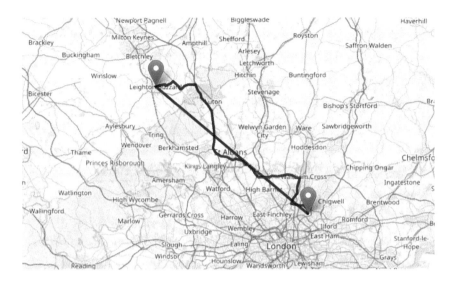

Google map showing the distance as the crow flies, which is 37.311 miles

If you go across the River Ouzel, you come to Linslade where the train station and the swimming pool are. Both towns have a history which dates to the '*Early Man*'. Let me tell you a bit about the history of Leighton Buzzard and its neighbouring town, Linslade.

In prehistoric times, the man preferred to live amongst hills, so he was able to see approaching danger. If he needed water, he would come down into the wetter parts of the valley to the area where it needed to be crossed. This was made up by the River Ouzel, and this could have caused the site of Leighton and Linslade to be developed by a ford over the river (Walker, Baker-Bates, & Brown, 1984).

There was a track developed that was used for travelling from east to west passing through Luton and Eggington (a village just outside Leighton Buzzard) that crossed the Ouzel at the ford which was called *Yttingaford* (now known as Tiddenfoot). This track was known as *Thiodweg*. This road was later called the *Salters Way* or *Salt Lane* (Walker, Baker-Bates, & Brown, 1984). From the ford, it went west towards the present-day settlement of Wing in Buckinghamshire.

Next came the Iron Age. Leighton Buzzard and its neighbouring town, Linslade, didn't escape this. There have been *burial urns* that were discovered in the sandpits near the Tiddenfoot ford. The people who were buried here were probably from nearby (Walker, Baker-Bates, & Brown, 1984). These people were farmers who created tools that allowed them to work the fields. They found the iron plough didn't wear out so fast and gave them a deeper furrow that meant they had a better chance at growing a good crop and building better living conditions (Walker, Baker-Bates, & Brown, 1984).

The Iron Age tribe who lived in the area around Leighton Buzzard were called the *Catevellauni* (Walker, Baker-Bates, & Brown, 1984). But in 43AD, their way of life was interrupted by the arrival of the Roman Legions. Near to Leighton Buzzard, there is a road which is the A5, also known as *Watling Street,* which is a road that extends from London to Holyhead in Anglesey. The Romans began constructing paved roads shortly after their invasion in 43 AD. During the rebuilding of St Mary-le-Bow by Christopher Wren following the Great Fire, the London part of the Watling Street was rediscovered. Modern-day excavation of the site puts its construction to the winter from AD 47 to 48 (Various, Watling Street, 2015). It originally started at Richborough on the English Channel to a natural ford in the Thames at Thorney Island near Westminster to a site near Wroxeter, where it split. The western continuation went onto Holyhead while the northern bit went to Chester and then onto the Picts in Scotland (Various, Watling Street, 2015).

Anyway, where was I? The villagers at the Leighton Ford, no doubt became used to their new rulers (Walker, Baker-Bates, & Brown, 1984). They began to make pottery in a new style copied from the Romans, which some of these pots from this time have been found at the site (Walker, Baker-Bates, & Brown, 1984).

Let us skip a few years, and then we can get to the Middle Ages. This was where a new menace threatened our shores. William, the Duke of Normandy, brought his reign to the shores in 1066 AD and invaded to lay claim to the throne of Edward the Confessor. In the Autumn of 1066, after his victory at Hastings, his army marched up from the coast and along the Icknield Way seizing the royal manors of Leighton, Luton and Houghton Regis, as well as the towns of Bedford and Aylesbury and King Harold's estate at Westoning (Walker, Baker-Bates, & Brown, 1984).

CHAPTER 4

Mid-twenties

*Think like a wise man but communicate
in the language of the people.*

—WILLIAM BUTLER YEATS

RIGHT, BACK TO MY LIFE AS THIS IS AN AUTOBIOGRA-
PHY, NOT A HISTORY BOOK! So, let us recap, I have left education and was trying to get a job as an I.T. professional with no such
luck.

During this time, Afasic had closed the Activity weeks due to
not enough funding, which upset all the adults, so I decided to take
them over and set them up myself. So, for one weekend in the year,
I would bring all the guys who were on the activity weeks with me
to an area, and we would do things like, walking, visiting places, la-
ser quest, and more. We had friends and family who helped on the
weekends, mostly with cooking and cleaning. The first weekend that
I did was in Snowdonia, North Wales. We went and visited places and
even climbed to the halfway point of Snowdon. I did about four more
weekends after that. But, unfortunately, it became too expensive, and

my Mother was paying for it as I didn't manage to organise myself quickly enough to get more people on it. I regret to this day have that happening.

Studying and Work

With no luck in becoming an I.T. professional, I decided to me become a lifeguard. During this time, I tried to self-teach JavaScript to improve on the language, but I became lazy and lacked focus. After a few years, that all changed though.

While at Tiddenfoot, I entered myself to become a swimming teacher and did a week's course on the subject. The reason why I did this was I wanted to try something new and thought that I could be a good swimming teacher. I was also getting bored with lifeguarding and wanted to spread my wings, so to speak. The course was done at another swimming pool over in Aylesbury, Buckinghamshire and consisted of practical and theory with an exam at the end of the course. In the course, we had to create our own lesson plans (this was unfortunately difficult for me) and then use the plans to teach it to the kids. For example, I had three different levels of kids, beginner, intermediate and advanced. The beginners, I had to write a lesson plan for them which allowed them to the lesson easily, but to learn the technique of the stroke, e.g. Front Crawl, and then have a little 'game' at the end of the lesson. The next class, intermediate class, was a bit easier for me, as they already somewhat knew how to swim, but we still needed to explain the techniques of the strokes and include a cooldown such as a game of some sort. Lastly, was the advanced class, this was my favourite, and the easiest as they knew how to swim, and they only needed to get told if they were doing something wrong. Here the end bit was teaching them diving and telling them where to improve on their swimming. The course materials, which were mainly session sheets were complex for someone with DLD to understand, and I struggled to write them out, so, unfortunately, didn't pass the course. I did learn a lot, though.

One thing I did learn was that you should never let one of your students jump into the pool with straight legs. That's not the end of the story. I got curious to know why, and one evening around Christmas time, when the pools were closed, and the lifeguards could go swimming. We were in the variable based pool[13], and one end was deep, and the other shallow, I remembered what the tutor had said and got curious again and jumped in. Fortunately, I did walk out, but I wouldn't recommend it as its bloody well hurts! I am paying for it now as I have swelling on the spine.

CHAPTER 5

Early Thirties

*Growing up in a group home, and with an undiagnosed
learning disability to boot, the odds of success were not
on my side. But when I joined the high school football team,
I learned the value of discipline, focus, persistence,
and teamwork - all skills that have proven vital to my
career as a C.E.O. and social entrepreneur.*

—DARELL HAMMOND

SO, AFTER I WAS AT TIDDENFOOT AS A LIFEGUARD FOR
10 YEARS, I got bored and started to focus on what I would like to
do in the future. I started to have another look at the JavaScript book
and concentrated on getting it into my head.

Self-teaching Web development

Once my mother had seen this, she asked if I really would like to do
this and would I study hard. I replied with a 'yes', and she suggested
that I should find an evening class in Web Development which I did

at Milton Keynes College. I attended it and passed the class. During this evening class, I learnt Dreamweaver and how to build a website, as my course at Barnfield College, but I was a lot better at it as I had learnt about design throughout the years by going to museums with my Mother and looking at books with the design. I think that it was just so she could get me into art, but it stayed in my mind. I worked hard at it and built a website off the back of the evening class, which did go up on the Internet.

My mother could see I was very interested in Web development, so she suggested I find a degree course at University, which turned out to be the foundation degree in web development. She could see that I was getting bored after being a lifeguard for ten years and I had started to self-teach myself JavaScript again and she could see that I was dedicated to changing my career and would work hard.

The course taught me how to code and build websites using HTML[14], CSS[15], and JavaScript[16], as well as other web technologies, such as databases and Java.

I continued to work hard at it and got better at web development and for the two years that the course ran for, I worked hard, and it paid off. I received a 2.2 and went off to the University of Derby.

When I went for an open day at the university, my mother and I were so impressed with the university, I said to her that I wanted to attend the University (my other choices were: *Brighton, Sussex, UEA, Leicester* (UEA and Leicester turned me down) and Sussex and Brighton accepted me, but I turned them down).

University of Derby

So, I was now at the University of Derby to study. What was my subject, and why did I study it? Well, it was initially going to be *BSc Internet Computing* as they didn't have Computer Science when I first attended. That course came much later. I had done okay, but not enough to go onto the next year straight away because I failed some of the modules. The next course I took was Information Technology as they had cancelled the BSc Internet Computing Course. In this course, there was some overlap with Internet Computing in my first years, such as modules on programming, computer fundamentals and web development. Web development has always been my favourite aspect of IT.

I hear you asking what web development is. Well, before you ask, it has nothing to do with spiders! But it is to do with computing. It is building a website that sits on the Internet for everyone to see. Let me break it down further for the people who are slightly lost here.

When you want to buy something, like food for your weekly shop, you can walk down to the supermarket and pick out your groceries and then go to a cashier to pay them. Or you can boot up your computer to shop online at one of the many supermarkets who have an online presence. To have this, the supermarket needs a website to be *developed* by someone who is experienced in building or developing websites. This job usually falls at the feet of a web developer. There are two sorts of people who build websites: a *web developer* or a *web designer*. The web developer is usually the person who builds a website just by code, while the web designer designs the website to make it look pretty. So, I feel that I am the web developer as I hand-code everything. It isn't easy, but in life, nothing is easy. Web development can be hard work because you must focus on many different concepts and be confident that you can piece together all the different aspects.

In the course, I have found that programming was the hardest. We had to learn a programming language which was developed by the Software Giant – Microsoft – called C# (pronounced as *C Sharp*). This language is based on the languages called C, C++ and Java. This language can be used to build websites (ASP.NET), operating systems and much more. I found it not very easy to learn because when I attended Derby, I hadn't ever come across the language before. So, I tried everything to continue learning the languages that were put in front of me. Thus, I continued building and revamping my website with the technologies that I was learning.

My website was the same as it was when I was at Milton Keynes College doing the evening course. It is about spreading awareness of this disability; hopefully, as will this book. I redesigned it to keep it fresh and to practice the skills that I have learnt. Like with everything, practice makes perfect. Building the website is also useful as I'm able to keep people up to date on the work that I do for Afasic, and it also keeps me up to date with a new way of coding the website. But mainly, it is an extra awareness for the charity, and every little bit helps them!

My lessons were built up with lectures, lessons and homework. The University had about ten lecture theatres (these were lecture theatres that we used, there were a lot more than that). They were a mixture of actual lecture theatres where the seats were in a tier up to the back of the hall. And then there were other lecture theatres that were just classrooms. In this structure, I preferred the lessons and homework as I could practice the subjects (especially if it was programming). My Mother always said that if you don't practice something, you never will get good at anything. That is so true. Web developers practise the skills that they need every day because they are building websites every day. I didn't enjoy essays, but it would have been even worse if I hadn't had the use of my computer. It was fairly fast as I can touch-type also.

Get Ahead

'Get Ahead' is a week-long forum where disabled students could be gently eased into the University life, and they had 'Mentors' to help them along the way if they had any trouble. This was very useful as a University can be very daunting and scary at times. Anyone who had a disability of some description could go along a week before the 'moving in weekend' came and meet other disabled students who were in the same boat. There were all kinds of disabilities, ranging from Dyslexia to autism, from DLD to deafness. Unfortunately, the biggest disability that was at the University was Dyslexia. With it being widely known, due to the press it receives, they could accommodate for it. While on the other hand, they couldn't quite accommodate speech and language impairment such as mine. I became a tutor of the disability for the support personnel.

There were a variety of different people, and I became good friends with two people from the group. One was deaf, and the other one was dyslexic. At University, we didn't do much with each other, sometimes met up. But we have kept in touch with each other via Facebook. I also met my predecessor for the post of Disabled Students Officer. And I met up with him quite a lot due to him teaching me a lot about the post.

Did Get Ahead help me? Yes, it did. I could understand how the University worked, and although I was homesick for the first year of my university life, it did help that I could go and get help if I needed it. I had been introduced to the support department of the University, and together we could get the much-needed help that I craved for in my course. So, yes, it did help. I think that all universities around the country should have this support group unless they do have it already.

CHAPTER 6

University Life

That's what university life is all about.
Challenging, questioning, enjoying good people
and good friends, and pushing yourself to the limit.

—David Robinson

UNIVERSITY LIFE IS AN EXPERIENCE. It is meant to be the best time of a person's life. It sure is. I had a great time at my university and made a lot of friends through it, only after the second year, though. I miss it, but I keep in contact with a lot of people through social media.

Freshers

When you're starting a new University, they always contain a 2-week event where they help you to make friends, find your way around the university and join a society and/or sports club. This is called *Freshers*. This happens in every university up and down the country. Freshers happen at the beginning of the University year (depending on when the courses started, for my University, this was September and January).

When I got myself sorted out, I got involved with the Freshers parties (or at least some of them) and met the Student Union resident photographer called Ben Martin. I became good friends with him, and we are still in touch with each other through Facebook. Although I'm not a photographer, (I usually point, snap and pray that the photos will end up looking good which I'd say 40% of the time they do), I was interested in what he took and where he could go to get photos of the drunken students! The Student Union used to have a street party in one of the streets of Derby town centre, and we could have a drink in any of the bars on that street. I thought that this was the best one as it was outdoors, and you didn't get hot as you would be getting if you were indoors. During this time of the street party, Ben managed to take a photo of another friend of mine with a friend of his what I didn't realise until I saw the photo of the two of them after university that the girl was Libby and I had been standing right next to Ben at the time. We weren't dating at that point, but it was not long afterwards. When I saw it, she was talking to me about the photo, and the penny dropped, and I told her that I remembered Ben taking the photo.

Before I attended university, I got into Archery at a local club to my home. I find Archery very enjoyable and relaxing. Unfortunately, I am unable to do archery while I am here in London now due to travelling as there isn't an archery club near to where I am living. At University, I managed to join the Archery club, and we practised in the sports hall and went to competitions. When I went to the competitions, I didn't do all that badly. Not as well as some of the others, but in my thoughts, I was there for the enjoyment. I didn't do many competitions as I was more interested in the sports hall practice. I feel that was better as I could shoot off some arrows to relax and have other members of the archery club look in awe at the bow (and at some points even try it – with me keeping a close watch over them).

The Halls

My university has got 3 Universities – two in Derby and one in the beautiful town of Buxton in the heart of the Peak District. It also has eight halls – seven in Derby and one in Buxton.

My halls were quite big (not the biggest) and I was with a mixture of young and mature students. They were a nice bunch, and still, I keep in touch with through social media. The rooms in my halls were a mixture of large and en-suite rooms. The ones that I was in weren't en-suite. We had a shared bathroom which consisted of just a shower (in some halls, I seem to remember that we had a bathroom with a shower and a bath in them) and a shared kitchen. We also had a common room where you could watch TV or a DVD, play pool or collect your post. I didn't use it much except collecting my post and any meetings that the Hall Manager gave.

Living in halls, it was a good time as we had to fend for ourselves, by cooking, buying food, but also if we needed any help the Hall Manager was there to give it to us. I have just mentioned the name 'Halls Manager' twice and haven't explained who he or she is. The *Halls Manager* is someone who looks after the Halls, such as mine and keeps anyone who didn't live in halls (such as non-students) off the premises. The one I had was very good at that as he was a retired police officer of the Derbyshire Constabulary. That's right; Halls Managers come from all walks of life. At the beginning of the university year, the Halls would have a meeting, and it was the Hall Manager to give it. They'd go through what you could and could not do, where you'd get the post, who was your Halls Rep (these were students whom you go to if you had a complaint and they'd take it back to the Student Union. They also took new students down to the Student Union's parties) and where you'd go to pay for your halls.

Sometimes, the university halls would do a barbeque for the students to bond and get to know each other. This happens at certain universities across the UK. Unfortunately, as far as I knew, this wasn't my university. At least I didn't hear of any barbeques happening at any of the halls. We had a barbeque on the terrace at the Student Union during Freshers or special occasions which were awesome.

I am not much of a party animal, unlike most university students. I preferred a quiet night in doing my coursework or a film at the cinema. I sometimes went to a pub with a friend of mine who lived in the halls (then later a house) and to the cinema. But with the cinema, she liked to talk through the film and pausing the film if she didn't understand it, which wasn't possible with the cinema. We mainly went to the pub overall and just sat over our drinks talking about random stuff and what she'd like to do when she graduated.

I remember when she and I were walking into town, and she received a call on her mobile. As we walked down the street together, she tapped me on the arm and mouthed "Where is my phone. We need to go back to the Halls, so I can get my phone as I've forgotten it." I gave a puzzled look as she had her phone to her ear "Erm, mate, you are talking on it" I replied. She looked at me and with a very embarrassed look realised. I literally fell about laughing that it made the caller wonder what all the noise was. My friend relayed it back, and they also fell about laughing. Just trust me when I tell you that she wasn't blond!

My favourite bit from the Halls was that we could stay for all our time at University. I stayed in halls the whole three years, as I couldn't find a group who I felt comfortable getting a house with.

Student Union

During my time at the university, I met the Disabled Students Officer through Get Ahead, and we became friends. After the first year, he saw that I had difficulties settling down into the university life and started to talk to me about doing things for the Union, and as the Union Elections were coming up, he suggested that I should run for the position of Disabled Students Officer. I found out that you were able to only run for two years and he had been in his second year, so was looking for someone to take it over. So, I decided to asked questions about what it entailed and later found out that I was the only one who showed an interest in it. With this in mind, I put my name forward to become the next Disabled Students Officer and ran for the position. Unfortunately, I found out that my predecessor received a lot of bad feedback about me, and the people behind the feedback wouldn't support me. Although with that said, I had successfully won the vote and therefore became the next Disabled Students Officer. I decided that I should become a DSO to highlight the Hidden Disabilities, such as DLD and thought it would be good on the CV. I had the chance to create (or run existing) campaigns which showed the difficulties of disabilities across the spectrum. My predecessor started a highly successful campaign, which I continued called the 'H' Campaign. This showed that more disabilities met the eye. There were disabilities, such as dyslexia, DLD, mental illness, and more. When I first saw it, I was literally bowled over by it as my disability is a hidden disability and some people do not believe that I have a disability until I start talking, then they still don't believe me or think that I have a stutter. The H campaign was an attempt to get people to make people aware of other types of disability, such as dysphasia, and start a conversation about them.

With this post of being the *Disabled Students Officer (DSO)*, I could go and speak at the Union Council, and if any policies were going through, I could vote for them. I decided my aim would also be to liven things up a bit. Well, there was one Union Council that I was at where the Academic President kept on jumping at and talking or blocking policies going through. He decided that he'd like to bring his section forward, as we were going to go for a break if he didn't, and the chair asked him to put his reasoning forward and asked if anyone was against it. I instantly put my hand up and was called to put my 'against speech' to the council: 'Okay, we have heard the Academic Officer jumping up and down talking for the past few hours and I'm not sure if anyone is with me on this, but I feel that we should vote for the break to happen because I know I am tired of hearing his voice and need a break.' I received a standing of ovation, and the vote went through as us wanting a break. With that, I sort of became the comedian of the council and livened it up.

Recently, Libby reminded me of a mutual friend of ours saying "…although Damo is pretty quiet, everyone knows that if he starts speaking, you need to shut up and listen because whatever he is about to say will be hilarious!" This I can say is true, because I gained a lot of friends through my work as a Disabled Students Officer with help from the Law Society as well as just generally. I could easily walk into the Student Bar, and if I saw the head chef, he would look at me and say to the person who's serving me 'He'll want an Academy Burger and diet coke' before I had said anything. Eventually, everyone who worked behind the bar knew my order.

One best part of this time was when we descended onto the Student Bar, and we had our special seats where we would sit every day. Before I go any further, let me describe our student bar. We had a bar where down the left side were booths and then if you move to the centre, it was high tables with stools around them, and then you get the bar. We also had a stage where events for the students' nights were placed, such as DJs, Lesbian, Gay, Bisexual, and Transgender (LGBT) Talent Show (I was an on-off member of this society as I came out as gay, but then later realized that I was bisexual), and more. We also had a terrace.

Well, as you know, I gained quite an of friends through being a DSO, and we would all meet up in the bar. We would occupy a booth and stay there for the length of time which we chose. I could walk into the bar, order a drink, and then sit in the booth. If no-one was there, then I'd place a message on Facebook and was guaranteed that someone would turn up within 10 minutes. The group became *The Academy Crew*. It became quite a big group, and unfortunately, we were never affiliated with the Students Union because our aim would have been to drink, meet with friends, and have a break from work. Hardly a good aim for an academic society! I found it funny that there were so many of us that all the Freshers avoided us as we were big and very loud. There were about 30 at last count! Yup, I found it hilarious! Unfortunately, now I don't have that popularity. If I ever go up to Derby to visit and put it onto Facebook that I'm in town, no-one appears, but if a mutual friend of Libby's and mine invite people out, she'll get everyone to her. Oh well, such as life. I don't honestly mind; people know where I am if they want to see me!

It was at University that I met Libby. According to Libby, she fancied me from the first moment when I was giving a speech at the Union Council as part of my DSO post. As you have found out from reading this book, I enjoy humour, but I also enjoy deep conversations. With Libby, this was both in her. I found that she was very interesting, as well as funny. To this day, I still feel the same, and we have a lot of different and interesting conversations from what has happened during the day, to I.T and the future of I.T. as well as psychology. But, while we were at university, I got into a relationship with her, and it was to the shock and delight of the rest of the Academy Crew.

Ahh…the good times!

Summer 2012 and the Olympics

[Needs expanding and editing…massively]

Summer 2012 was the summer of many sports events in the UK, with the biggest one being the Olympics. Held in several areas with the majority being held in Stratford in East London, events here included the athletics and swimming. We also had the White-Water Rafting at a centre in Hertfordshire, as well as rowing down in Dorset on the south coast. The Government had promised that Summer 2012 would be the best summer that the UK would have with the Summer Games, and we would have the best Olympics. And it sure did deliver.

So, why am I writing about this? Well, let go back to September 2011, where my journey to this started.

At this point, I was at University, and we were told that someone from the company 'Bridging the Gap' was coming to the University to recruit students for the task of being security at the Olympics 2012. I instantly placed my name onto the line and started the journey to becoming a G4S security officer. We were told what we would expect, why the recruitment was happening and a lot more things which I can't remember at the time of writing this book. The official finally arrived at the University, and we started our initial training. We found out the history of the organisation, and who G4S is. At the time, they were required to recruit approximately 3,000 students for the Games (I'm not exactly sure on the number, but I do remember it was in the highs!)

At Derby College, we were based for our lessons in the Door Supervision courses. As I found out later in my life, the training that we got was a cut-down version of the actual course. Although, it did give me an insight into the qualification and got me doing the Games when it finally came around. We were taught how to stop someone from entering (in the scenario, it was a pub/nightclub) a building and how to restrain someone. We were also taught how to search for someone and their bags.

After about three weeks of doing this, we were required to marshal the streets for the Olympic Torch and stop people from running up to the torch! This point was fascinating as the torch was brought through Derby by a person called The Torch Bearer (usually a celebrity, e.g. we had the rapper, Will.I.am, running through a town in Devon called Taunton) and it was protected by 4 burly officers of the Metropolitan Police from London who stayed with it until it reached the Queen Elizabeth II Stadium in Stratford, London.

Finally, we were all deployed in our specific areas. Unfortunately, G4S totally messed the event up, so much that they reached the news outlets, like the BBC. There were a lot of students who never received their letter or phone call to say where they were getting placed. Fortunately for me, I called them every week up to the start date and was successful in getting placed. For me, I was placed at Greenwich, South London, and found out that I was not meant to be there. I found that G4S had sent me to the wrong place, and it was meant to be the Lee Valley White Water Centre, Hertfordshire. So, I spent one day and night at Greenwich and secured the O^2. This was still interesting as we had one area which was going down to a party boat blocked off, due to the Olympics getting set up and I had one persistent drunk guy always trying to get passed me, and I always stopped him and turned back. I think the Police was watching him as after about the fourth time of him pestering me, they came and picked him up (literally) and took him away. I was thankful for that as I didn't see him for the rest of the night. After that, I appeared at the White-Water Centre where I was a member of the patrol team, and we had to check the perimeters to see if they were all safe and that all the workmen were wearing IDs. This job was tiring but enjoyable. My team usually worked at night and were on our feet for quite a bit. Although we enjoyed the position, we certainly looked forward to going back to the hotel for a well-earned sleep at the end of the shifts.

What I noticed between the patrolling, we had a canteen where we had our breakfasts, lunches, and suppers and everyone who worked on the site at that time were there. We also could have it to get coffees and other hot drinks during the night. We were working alongside the Army, and when we went in for the breaks, it was G4S in one area, Police in another area, and Army in another area. What I mean is that we were very separate when we were on breaks, this is I thought was strange as were all on the same team, I think. But we still worked hard, and I ended up getting pneumonia after about week as it rained heavily during the night. I went to see Libby on one of my days off, and I didn't feel very well. I arrived at Walthamstow and threw up on the stairs on the way out of the underground, and then when I arrived at Libby's Mother's house, I basically told her what happened and went to bed, I threw up throughout the night and ended up in hospital the next day. I was in the hospital for a week, and they found out that I had pneumonia and I couldn't go back to the Olympics until I recovered.

I was released from the hospital and was ordered by my Mother to be returned home that day – she even sent a taxi to get me. The taxi arrived while we were having lunch and I had to rush it as I also had Mother on the phone telling me that she wanted me back immediately. Trust me when I say that Libby wasn't happy!

After a few weeks of recovery, I was well enough to go back to the Olympics, but unfortunately, I wasn't placed. The experience that I got in those few days of working at the White-Water Centre will always stay with me, and I won't ever forget it.

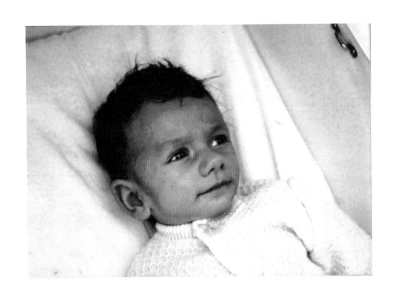

Me as a baby

Me and my dad

Me learning to walk

Whenever my dad had his lightbox on,
I liked to go over to him and turn it off

My parents use to say to me "Damian, where's your tummy'
and I'd lift up my top and point to it.

Me and my houseparent at my school's sports day

I got Pooh bear for Christmas when I was at my grandmother's house, and I was
drinking tea and he decided to steal some of it,
or was I sharing it? You decide.

My Mother, me and my cousin at my grandmother's. Think that this was
Christmas. We usually all descend onto her house for Xmas

Me at an awards ceremony for the Students Union

I use to horse ride, and here I am doing a gymkhana.

Some of the choir at the Afasic Christmas Concert (Credit: Greg Keeling)

A speaker from Moore House School at the Christmas Concert
(Credit: Greg Keeling)

Me as a host at the Christmas Concert
(Credit: Greg Keeling)

Sir Derek Jacobi at the Christmas Concert (Credit: Greg Keeling)

Figure 18: The hosts, and my understudy (Credit: Greg Keeling)

Robert Meadmore at the Christmas Concert (Credit: Greg Keeling)

The Brighton and Hove Signing Choir (Credit: Greg Keeling)

The HRH Duchess of Gloucester and Afasic's CEO, Linda Lascelles (Credit: Greg Keeling)

HRH Duchess of Gloucester, Director of Fundraising, Mark Thompson and CEO of Afasic, Linda Lascelles (Credit: Greg Keeling)

Elaine Delmar at the Christmas Concert (Credit: Greg Keeling)

CHAPTER 7

After University

When you hear the word 'disabled,' people immediately think about people who can't walk or talk or do everything that people take for granted. Now, I take nothing for granted. But I find the real disability is people who can't find joy in life and are bitter.

—Teri Garr

During the summer of 2012, while I was at the Olympics, I was still studying. I returned to Uni in September only to find I was not able to continue with my studies. I felt that I failed my parents, who paid a lot of money for me to be at University, and the tutors, as well as myself. Remember me telling you if we got into trouble with Mr Holmes at my school; he'd give us the silent treatment? Well, that's what happened with my Mother. I could see that she was disappointed, and I felt this until the day that she died. Anyway, going back to the story, when a tutor told me that he didn't think I could do computing, it was like as if I had been shot in the heart. It destroyed me. So, I had to do something about it, and that was that I vowed to prove to everyone who doubted that I could do I.T. that I could do it (I even had to prove to myself that I could do it) and worked hard to self-teach I.T.

I enrolled myself on the *edX: Introduction to Computer Science* given by Harvard University, which was a free course. This course taught me different areas of the Computer Science field, such as Artificial Intelligence (Ai), programming in C++ and much more. It wasn't easy, but I managed to complete it. In this course, I found that the topic of Artificial Intelligence very interesting. This still is with me now. Look at the world now; we are heading to a future that will have robots, self-driving cars. We have the latter already, but in the form of the London Underground – the Victoria Line was the first underground train which was fully autonomous, and when it was first implemented, it had no driver. But, the users of the service were so scared of it, they demanded that there should be a driver just in case something goes wrong. Now, on the Underground, there are quite a few of the trains that are autonomous, like the Dockland Light Railway (DLR). I have even looked to see how I could implement AI into my website, but I couldn't figure out what I would want it to do. So, that may well be implemented at a later stage once I learnt it and figured out what I would want to do with it.

Artificial Intelligence is an amazing phenomenon. With every year that passes, computer nerds are getting ever closer to the breakthrough which will give us AI forever. It is still in early stages, but we are more advanced with it than we were 20 years ago. We have AI implemented in hundreds of technologies where we didn't expect would have it when the thought of AI started. But there is that initial thought from people who don't understand it: Will robots take over the jobs of humans? I don't think that it will. It will give more jobs to humans as they will need jobs in different areas of work.

Sorry, I digress; afterwards, I started to work on the MCSD: Web Applications qualification. I worked hard on this, but this wasn't easy. I had to learn all about HTML, CSS and JavaScript. These are the three languages (well HTML is what is called a '*markup language*' which is a language that any web page must have to make it work. Without it, it's useless as there's no web page). CSS is what is called a '*styling language*' which allows web developers and designers to create pretty websites. Without it, all you'll see is a lot of writing without any formatting, basically what you'd see if you turn CSS off in the options. JavaScript is the only actual language that is in this section of the MCSD. There is more advanced code that appears in the other modules. (More about this later in the chapter).

I went back up to Derby to see my friends and Libby at some points of her last year, which was enjoyable. I also could catch up on what's been happening to everyone. I tried to get into the University of Bedfordshire to repeat the degree but was unable to get the funding for it. So, by this point, Libby had graduated in BSc (Hons) in a Psychology course, and we moved in together for a time at my parents' house as I was looking after my Mother while my father was in America.

After a few weeks, I had been chatting with a friend of mine, called Phil who was a Sound engineer and computer technician, before Libby finished the course, and he suggested for a time while we look for a place of our own, she could rent his spare bedroom. Libby was happy with this suggestion, so moved in. I went and stayed some nights with her.

In September 2012, we were engaged. I bought her a ring which I found out later had our birthstones – Diamond for her, and an amethyst which was my birthstone.

Moving to London

After two months of being in Leighton Buzzard, Libby was unable to find any job that suited her, so she decided that she wanted to move to London to get a job. London is an ideal place to find a job as there are a lot more opportunities, and it was also Libby's hometown. I was reluctant to move as I was used to my hometown. But throughout the summer and having seen where she lived in 2012 at the Olympics, she made me realise that not all of London is a bad place. There are some nice parts.

We moved to London in September 2013, and we found that finding a job in London was quite easy, unfortunately, though, I was back to being a lifeguard, and Libby was doing the door-to-door selling.

Finding Places to Live

Finding a place to live in London when the prices of houses or the rent are so high, is not easy. But fortunately, we found one. We lived in a one-bedroom flat where the bedroom was so small, it could just fit a double bed in it with an inch around it, and you couldn't even swing a poor cat in it. If you ever tried to, you probably get hurt by the cat scratching you! The kitchen was a small kitchen with all the usual utilities in it, but even then, you had trouble opening the washing machine and oven at the same time!

After we had been in this flat, we had to leave as the owners of the flat (our landlady and landlord) wanted to sell it. We were fortunate to find a flat which was bigger than our first flat. We could even open the washing machine and the oven at the same time! It did have its flaws which were that the flat was a bit mouldy and not enough storage. But the flat was big enough for us. The other benefit was that the landlord and the neighbour that we had were both very friendly.

A Town Called Walthamstow

In this section, I am going to talk about the history of Walthamstow, and as before, you are welcome to skip to the next section of this chapter on Page 109 if you prefer to know all about me, but I promise, this is the last history insert!

In this section, I am going to talk about the history of Walthamstow, how it evolved, and how Libby and I came to live here.

Walthamstow is a town on the outskirts of east London. It lies 13.9 miles away from Victoria, with one of the longest markets in the country. However, it hasn't always been like this. Libby recalls a family friend telling her about her house being in the middle of a field in the 1940s, and plenty of the houses having grounds, like weekend getaways from London.

The town was recorded in the doomsday book in 1086AD as two different settlements, High Home (modern-day Higham Hill) and Walthamstow. High Home may have alternatively been called Tunmanhille, and since it was less densely populated, paid its taxes to Walthamstow. As the years went by, High Home was absorbed into

Walthamstow, which closely resembles the borough today, (Mander, 2001).

Historians are unsure where the name Walthamstow came from. It could be that it evolved from the word Wilcuma, which would mean the full name translated to "The place where strangers are welcome" (Mander, 2001). I certainly felt welcomed the first time I came down to see Libby.

In the centre of Walthamstow Village, there is a museum, The Vestry House Museum. As expected, back in 1813 it was the vestry room of the parish workhouse, and the location for the local councillors to meet. Here, they discussed many issues, including the collection of taxes (Mander, 2001). The Vestry House is now used as a local archive and museum, which is free to the public and hosts local events, such as weddings.

Until 1878 Walthamstow was one of the Essex parishes, counted under the Forest of Waltham or Epping. The forest had been preserved during the reign of the Tudors as a royal hunting reserve. The landscape during Tudor times, as now in some parts, was a mixture of woodland, and open plains, allowing deer to roam free throughout the area. Enclosures could also be made by royal license (Mander, 2001). A great visit if you would like to see evidence of this hunting pedigree, is the Queen Elizabeth's Hunting Lodge, in Chingford, just on the edge of Epping Forest.

In 1642, hunting was paused during the English Civil War, and in 1653 Parliament legislated to sell the entire forest. Fortunately, it was decided that the land could be put to better use. Charles II resumed the right to hunt in 1660, which continued until 1714 when George I ascended the throne.

Some hunting did continue, though. Londoners had been granted the right to hunt in early medieval times, and this Easter Chase, which took place during the spring, continued until 1882, (Mander, 2001).

Unfortunately, Libby tells me that many of the species that were hunted in the area were driven out during the time. Deer and Boar were common at the time but are rarely seen nowadays. Although I recently read that there had been a potential sighting of boar burrows or nests, which could be a sign of the return of the wild boar to Greater London.

One of the oldest places in Walthamstow must be St Mary's Church, right in the heart of the village. There are graves in the surrounding area that date from 1200. It played a part in charity, education, and spiritual activities since the time it was built, (Mander, 2001), but unfortunately, there is no certain date ascribed to it. There has been a church building on Church Hill before 1147, and it is likely that somewhere between 1103-1130 one of the de Tony family oversaw the parish, but we cannot be certain, (Mander, 2001).

Another important part of Walthamstow's history is that William Morris lived here in the mid-19th century. His house is open to visitors and is located within a large park. Here you can see some of the more famous designs he created, as well as an exhibition space for more contemporary art and design. I once went with Libby, during summertime. She was wearing a striped dress and almost disappeared into a chaise lounge which was covered in the same material. That certainly got my Irlen's syndrome!

In the past few years, Walthamstow has given the world some well-known and not so well-known pop groups.

In 1962, a group called 'The Beaucrees' was formed. This was the first group to be formed, and in 2013, the decision to reform and hold several local gigs. They continue to play at local gigs across the Waltham Forest borough (Collier, 2014). The next band that that was formed was an unsuccessful band called East End Boyz. Unfortunately, they didn't get to the dizzy heights of stardom, unlike the next band East17. This band helped to put Walthamstow on the map. The band had hits like 'Stay Another Day', 'House of Love' and 'Steam' (Collier, 2014).

So, there you go, Walthamstow has quite a musical history under its belt. The house that Libby and I currently live in was used as a recording studio in the 1960s, so maybe I'll catch the musical bug!

Right, back to my life…

Working in a London Swimming Pool

Working in a swimming pool as a lifeguard can be quite stressful as you must put up with all the customers moaning at you that you are not doing a good job and children screaming because they want to talk to their friends who are at the other end of the pool. If you ever been to a swimming pool in London, then you will know what I mean. When I was used to a quiet pool which only saw about sixty swimmers on its busiest times, I was overwhelmed by the number in a London pool at its busiest time.

I started working at a pool near our flat in October 2013 and was thinking that it would be like Tiddenfoot, how wrong was I? It brought in customers not just from Walthamstow, but customers from the surrounding towns. On its busiest times, the pools were packed out by screaming kids, and adults who didn't like a lane to be taken out when we had Swim School in because they had no room. You had to have a whole new set of skills to lifeguard a packed-out pool like this.

What I found while lifeguarding at the London pools, compared to Tiddenfoot, was that if you saw a swimmer either playing dangerously (if it was a minor) or swimming dangerously (meaning if he or she couldn't care less if they caused an accident while they swam) then the lifeguard would have to call for the Duty Manager (DM) to get the swimmer out of the pool. Let me tell you a story about this situation, and I'll be giving you examples from Tiddenfoot as well with the story.

I was lifeguarding at the pool near my flat and one day, I saw a swimmer taking a swim school sausage (one of these floats that is long and cylindrical that allows a swimmer (usually a swim school swimmer) to wrap it under themselves for buoyancy) and swimmers in a public swimming session weren't allowed to use them as they were especially for the swim school lessons. I went and told her that she wasn't allowed, and she started up an argument with me and demanded to see the DM. I called for the DM and after a few minutes of him arriving, she was out of the pool and the centre.

While back in Tiddenfoot, if this happened, I wouldn't need the support of the DM, unless it was really necessary. I could go up to the customer, request for the float to be given to me, and if they started up an argument I could say 'Fine then, goodbye get out of my pool. And by the way, you're banned!!'. The DM was only asked to come to the poolside for me to tell them that the customer was banned as he or she was arguing with me and the DM would say 'Okay, what he says. Goodbye.' And we wouldn't hear from the customer ever again. Every centre and company are different, but it did take me by surprise when I found this out. I was expecting to go in and be my usual self with chucking people out, but oh nooo, I couldn't.

I had to return to my hometown for a bit to look after my ill cat while my father went off to America and after I had returned to London, I decided that I wanted to work where Libby worked. She was a Customer Service Advisor for the same company but down in South East London. So, the pool was quiet except when the Swim School® classes started. Swim School is in all swimming centres where they teach children how to swim. They go from Stage 1 all the way up to Stage 12. The younger age groups (Stages 1 to about 7) are the nosiest while the pre-teens up to mid-teens (about Stages 7 to 12) want to learn!

To get to the Centre, it was about a 3-hour journey from my house. But it was worth it as I was doing a job that I sort of enjoyed. I did find that there was a duty manager who didn't like me, but I have a knack of ignoring people who I don't want to know which I did with him.

Overall, I worked hard and put in my rescues when it was needed. At this point, with me being in the job the longest, I unofficially found that I had the respect from the duty managers to manage the team. And with this, the team was happy with me. Although, I continued to do what I needed to do and didn't act as 'the boss'. I think if I were at the centre full time, then I would have become a duty manager within months! I did have this chance, but unfortunately, I didn't go to work at the centre which was near my house. I wish I had, as it could have put me in good stead for the job that I'm doing now.

Every two years, a lifeguard needs to retake his or her qualification to see if they remember everything. And to learn new things if the Royal Life Saving Society UK has changed anything. For example, when I first started, you were only meant to do 15 chest press and two breaths in CPR, and now it's 30 chest press and two breaths (which is optional). Also, if you use an Automated External Defibrillator you were meant to be specially trained in it (i.e. if you were a DM, you could use it, but if you were a lifeguard, forget it). Now, if I went back to lifeguarding, I would have to retake the exam and do the course from scratch. I think that I could easily do it, but I would rather have a refresher.

Although, I am not looking to go back to this job as everything has changed and I would literally be starting from scratch in everything. It was good while it lasted, but you do need a change of scenery at some point in your life. I chose this to do the courses, such as the QA courses. This really stretched my mind, and I'm glad that I've done it…

CHAPTER 8

Courses with QA

*Success is no accident. It is hard work, perseverance,
learning, studying, sacrifice and most of all, love of what you
are doing or learning to do. Pele*

I hear you asking, *'what is QA?'* Well, this organisation is not anything
to do with Quality Assurance, but with training.

QA is a major training centre for IT, Business, and Leadership,
to name a few. With 30 years of experience, it has become to be the
number 1 training centre in the UK, if not, the world! Like with all
professional training, it doesn't come cheap. But you go to QA to get
an in-depth knowledge of the skills you would like to train in.

What would you like to train in? I.T? Well, they have several
courses to train in from Microsoft courses, such as the MCSD (more
information about this is coming up in the next section), Amazon
Web Services, Cisco (which is the largest computer networking organisation in the world) and a lot more. They can teach you anything.
It is the same with the other courses that are in other areas of work.

You attend the courses, either with a sketchy knowledge of the
area that you're training in or with a working knowledge. And you are

taught to have an underpinning knowledge to be able to pass an exam from the body that you're training in, for example, Microsoft.

MCSD: Web Apps

Sample code for HTML

MCSD: Web Apps, otherwise known as Microsoft Certified Solutions Developer: Web Applications, is a course that is created by the software giant. It has been created so developers can learn web development using Microsoft Technologies and Visual Studio®.

To gain the certification, you need to pass three exams which are:

* *HTML, CSS, and JavaScript*

  In this course, you learn how to write in HTML (as shown in figure X). The code that you write can be either easy or hard, depending on the level you are on. The graphic on the right is how the HTML5, CSS3 and JavaScript look like. HTM5 is a markup language and is the skeleton of a website. Without, you wouldn't see a site.

  HTML was born in 1993 by *Sir Tim Berners-Lee,* a British physicist who was working for *Conseil Européen pour la Recherché Nucléaire* (CERN, also known as European Organization for Nuclear Research) and over time, it grew and became more widely used. Along with HTML, came another markup code called *Cascading Stylesheet* (otherwise known as *CSS*) which is used for styling the website. In other words, it made the website look pretty. This markup is the second most important as it creates eye-candy for the user. In today's world, CSS allows you to format virtually anything, from tables to paragraphs, and it also allows you to create a website that is mobile-friendly as websites are now being created as mobile-first websites. The final language that you learn in this part of the course is JavaScript. This is an actual language and is widely used. It is a client-side language, meaning it is the language that is used on the user's computer. It is used for the behaviour aspect of the website. Need a button to do something when it's pressed? Well, JavaScript can do this. This is just a basic example of what JavaScript can do.

If you remember back in the 90s, the annoying pop-up boxes, this was created by JavaScript. Now there are standards that all developers must follow, and fortunately, pop-up boxes have virtually been wiped out.

In the next course that you need to take to get the certification is, ASP.NET MVC (shown figure 25). This is a server-side language that is created by Microsoft. This language uses C# (pronounced as *CSharp*) and all the usual markup languages and coding, such as the ones which were previously mentioned. ASP.NET was created in 2002 to allow developers to build dynamic websites and applications. MVC stands for Model, View and Controller.

The final course is to Microsoft Azure. This one allows the developer to put a website up onto the Internet using the server and create tougher security and even databases without downloading anything. Azure is what is called a 'Cloud Server' which means the server is on the servers in Microsoft Datacentres across the world.

```
List.aspx  List.aspx.cs  ProductsController.cs
Client Objects & Events                                                    ▼  (No Events)
   <%@ Page Language="C#" MasterPageFile="~/Views/Shared/Site.Master" Inherits="MyStore.View
   <asp:Content ID="Content1" ContentPlaceHolderID="MainContentPlaceHolder" runat="server">
       <h2>
           <asp:Literal ID="CategoryName" runat="server" />
       </h2>
       <ul>
           <asp:Repeater ID="ProductList" runat="server">
               <ItemTemplate>
                   <li>
                       <%# Eval("ProductName") %>
                   </li>
               </ItemTemplate>
           </asp:Repeater>
       </ul>
   </asp:Content>
```

Sample of ASP.NET MVC

After all this learning, you manage to get through the courses; you need to take the exams to get the certification.

This course isn't meant to be easy, but people can get through the exams relatively easily. But having DLD, and bad memory, it isn't easy at all. When I did the courses, I revised and then tried to take the exam and failed it. So, now, I am revising using books, Microsoft® Virtual Academy™, and other video learning websites. I hope to pass the exams soon, but I just wanted to focus on studying.

CHAPTER 9

Married life

Let the wife make the husband glad to come home
and let him make her sorry to see him leave.

—Martin Luther

WHO WOULD HAVE THOUGHT THAT THIS WOULD HAPPEN TO ME? I have gone through life with DLD and climbing mountains to just get to this stage. If someone came to me at the age of 20 and told me that I would be married in 20 years, I would have laughed at them and probably would have told them where to go. Why do I think this? Well, throughout my life, I have had relationships thrown back in my face. But, when I met Libby at University, we somehow clicked. We found that we enjoyed deep and meaningful conversations as well as films, although her favourite films are comedy films, which is excellent as I find comedy amazing!

We got together in the Summer of 2012, and it was to the joy of our friends that we got together. Well, that was *Facebook Official*, but how we got together was that we were in a deep conversation while walking back to her house, and we ended up continuing to chat at her house. And then it developed from there.

From there, the thought of getting engaged was long-time planning as I had to find the right ring for her. She gave me a mile-long list of jewels that she didn't like, but finally, I found a ring which suited both of us. It was a purple amethyst encrusted with diamonds. I found out that it was our birthstones, amethyst was mine, and the diamond was hers. At the time of me getting the ring, I had arranged to meet her at St Pancras (I had a meeting with RALLI (see Chapter X) in the morning), and I thought that I should get the ring beforehand.

Unfortunately, I had gone to a shop that didn't have the ring, and that made me late for Libby. If guns were like they are in America here, I think that I'd be dead as she was very upset and angry with me! Fortunately, I managed to calm her down and told her that I wasn't leaving her. Although, she told me a few months later, that she was ready to dump me when I appeared in front of her in Costa Coffee®. Luckily, I had appeared, and we continued our day of going to Stratford and having a good day where I eventually, managed to gain the ring and sat her down and proposed to her, and with that, she burst into tears and couldn't stop hugging me! Apparently, she didn't really want to say 'yes' straight off, but after a few days of mulling it over, we were on the road to the wedding. It wasn't anything romantic, I didn't get down on one knee and proposed (mainly because with my knees, I couldn't as I had damaged them a few years ago, and it's very hard for me to crouch or go down onto them nowadays).

When I decided that I wanted to get engaged with her, I didn't know what to do, how I should ask her. Therefore, I went down this route. Was I nervous? Of course, I was, anyone would be if he or she proposes to that special someone, male or female. I thought that Libby would say 'no' to me and when she saw the ring and didn't answer, I thought that it was a no and did take the ring back.

After she said yes, I was delighted and went home and told my Mother, and all she said was 'I thought that you would be'. What a conversation killer! Eventually, I got it out of her that she was pleased, but it did upset me that she said something like that. But my Mother was like that. She very rarely showed any emotion, and it wasn't easy to see what she felt about things. To compare her to a fictitious person, I'd go with *Captain Holt* from *Brooklyn 99*, the team could never read him, and I could never read my Mother.

Like with all couples, we do have our differences; I find that I misunderstand with what she says, and I am sure that it frustrates her that I misunderstand her, so it can't be easy for her. But three years down the line, she continued to stay with me and became my wife.

The Wedding

About a year after we got engaged, we decided on a date for the wedding. It was going to be September 6, 2014. The planning of the wedding wasn't going to be easy, and those people who are reading this autobiography which has gone through the planning stage of the wedding will know what I mean. The organising of finding the place of where to get married, the invite list, the alcohol, the food, the music, etc., etc. It wasn't easy. First, we had to decide who should come, who should be the bridesmaids/best man. Fortunately, the latter was easy to find as we had friends from University who jumped at the chance to be the best man and bridesmaids for us. The next problem that we ran into was where we should get married. We initially wanted a pagan wedding, but unfortunately, that didn't happen in London. So, we decided on a registry office, and when we went there for an interview, we were very disappointed in the look of the registry office. Fortunately, we had been told about *The Vestry House Museum*[17] by Libby's Mother, which we went to look at and we were very impressed with it as the Museum had a Community Hall out at the back which could hold 80 people and we could have the use of the garden.

The bride and groom signing the wedding book

So, we had the bridesmaids and best man, the hall and the registrar…what else could go wrong? Nothing as we could see? We made up a list of everyone we wanted to come to the wedding and went off to order the cake and the alcohol. We looked in at a cake shop in Chingford and nearly decided on buying a 'Cheshire Cat' Cake. But we decided against it and got a normal three-tier Madeira cake. We then went to another shop, just to browse, and the shopkeeper couldn't do enough for us when we told her that we were getting married. Then finally, we ordered the wine.

Now, this brings us to the invites; as I said, nothing could go wrong after the registry office (although that wasn't massive). I found an online company that did invites and would even send them. They were in our price limit too. Looked good, sounded good, and were based in France. Hmm, now looking at it, I should never have trusted a company which said they sent invites when they were based in another country.

So, I gathered all the addresses and names of the people who wanted to come and entered it into the website and paid over the money and waited for the invites to be sent. Then the disappointing news came in. Half of our friends and families weren't getting the wedding invites. This concerned me a lot, and I instantly got onto the company to complain, and they sent out the invites again to the ones who didn't get it. Unfortunately, that didn't happen as they still didn't get the invite. We then decided just to do it by word of mouth and fortunately, that worked.

Unfortunately, through the days leading up to the wedding, Libby received some bad news about her bridesmaids. All of them but one dropped out. This broke her heart as it was too close to the wedding for her to find other bridesmaids. But fortunately, my best man didn't drop out, and Libby was settled.

So, now the days brought us to the day before the wedding. We had Libby's bridesmaid, called Amy, and my best man called Bob with us. We went to the community hall and decorated it with balloons, and when we were about to leave, two women who worked at the museum saw what we did and said "Oh you can't leave that overnight. It'll set the alarms off!" so we had to take everything that was stuck up on the walls down and put them up in the morning. Next morning, we put everything back up.

Libby had a 'hen party', but I didn't have a stag night. Bob and I stayed in drinking, watching films and chatting. Next morning, we had to collect the food which Libby and I ordered it from one of the supermarkets. And I also got a close shave from the barbers. Overall, I was terrified that more bad luck would come to us, but fortunately, it didn't.

The hour of the wedding approached, and Bob and I waited by the doors for everyone to come in, and a few came, and I thought with the farce of the invites only about 30 people would attend. I had to go off to have another interview with the registrar, just to clarify what was going to happen and how a wedding worked, and when I went back to the hall, everyone had turned up. We even had people standing up at the back! I was amazed, and the nerves started to set in reality.

The music went on (albeit, the wrong one. I had threatened to play *Carmina Burana* by Carl Orff, instead of a Buddy Holly's song. But by the time the wedding had arrived, I had forgotten and put *Led Zepplin* on, which I think Libby told me that the song was all about someone breaking up with their loved one and I think it was called '*Babe I'm Gonna Leave You*', but can't really remember) and waited which felt an eternity for Libby to arrive. Then the registrar started to speak and welcome everyone to the wedding, and I thought, 'Hold on, Libby isn't here, you need to wait for her.' And then I looked at the person who was next to me and then at the registrar still thinking that Libby wasn't next to me 'C'mon miss, you need to wait for Libby, this person isn't…wow, this is Libby…' at this point, I had looked again and realised. Libby was dressed in a purple dress with a grey jacket that only went over the shoulders (as shown in Figure 26). She looked amazing, and I hadn't recognised her. I had to say my bit and ended up just saying 'Whaaa?' as I had got lost over what I was meant to repeat. Fortunately, I had explained to the registrar that I had a speech and language disability before the wedding, and she repeated it but at a pace where I could manage it.

Libby, on the other hand, when I said my bit, was in tears. I couldn't believe how much she cried throughout the day! The community hall and garden nearly came to a filling point with everyone's tears! Any more tears, we would have a swimming wedding!

After the ceremony, it was party time, or as some people call it – paarrrtttaaayyy time! We set about eating, chatting, drinking, and then repeat! Bob and Libby's Mother made speeches and then repeated the bit that I just mentioned. Bob's speech was about his friend who he was also the best man for and in German (thinking that he was okay in German) said the totally wrong thing. It embarrassed him as well as his friend. One of Libby's friend knew German and laughed at the joke before everyone else, realised that no-one else was laughing, stopped, and then laughed again when the joke was said in English.

One of the guests, called Kim, did a Champagne pyramid which Libby and I had to take the first glass. We were both terrified of doing it as we weren't sure if it would knock the whole lot down. Fortunately, it didn't.

Like the other two people in this autobiography, I have asked Kim to write a piece to say how she met me, and how she found me:

"I first met Damo when we were both working at the leisure centre. He was lifeguarding whilst I was teaching swimming lessons. At first, he seemed very quiet and shy, and we didn't talk.

"One day, while I was teaching, I received news of Damo becoming unwell while lifeguarding the pool next door to where I was teaching. A few weeks later, I was working with the same Duty Manager who was on shift when Damo became unwell. I asked him how Damo was and was told that he was ok, and if I wanted to know how he was, I should add him on Facebook. So, I did.

"From there, we built up a really strong friendship and soon agreed to meet up, so we could talk in person.

"When I met with Damo, I was surprised to hear him speak, especially as I had never spoken to him face-to-face before. He was quite slow with his speech, and I then noticed he was wearing a hearing aid. I later found out that this was due to Damo suffering a stroke in the womb.

"Despite everything, I found Damo easy to talk to, and he has remained a very good friend of mine. He later introduced me to his, then, fiancé Libby who has also become a friend of mine.

"When Damo and Libby got married on 6th September 2014, it was very clear just how much they both meant to each other.

"This was then showed a few months later when Damo was taken into hospital a few months later. He was struggling to breathe and became dependent on oxygen for a short while. Both Libby and I were very worried; Damo however, remained optimistic throughout his whole time in the hospital and even when he was discharged.

"Throughout it all, he remained an inspiration through his high spirits. I'm so proud of how Damo has dealt with everything, and I'm glad he is a good friend of mine."

I would like to thank Kim for doing this for the book

Back to the wedding, at one point during the evening, Libby realised that she had a magic glass as when she finished the Prosecco, it was refilled, and she didn't see it being refilled. Her aunts did a brilliant job of getting the food onto the tables as well as keeping glasses refilled.

After we had finished with the Vestry House as there was a time limit on how long we could stay for (which was okay for us), we went to a local Italian restaurant, called *Nuovo Mondragone Restaurant*. The restaurant basically cut off half of the restaurant for us. There we continued to chat and enjoy ourselves. Finally, we ended at a local pub and drunk the night away.

The Honeymoon

In June 2014, Libby and I started to look where we could go to for our honeymoon. We both agreed that we wanted it to be a few months after the wedding and where we could sunbathe. So, we looked at the TUI (formerly known as *Thomson Holidays)* website, a UK travel company and found that we could go to somewhere in the Atlantic Ocean just off North Africa – i.e. to the beautiful island of Lanzarote. If you've never been to the Island, I would recommend it. It is a beautiful place, and I will explain more in a few paragraphs time!! We booked two weeks out in the Island of the Sun and in October 2014, we were on the flight at the early hours of the morning.

The night before we travelled out to Lanzarote, we decided to go and stay at a Premier Inn which was near to the airport, but I was meant to be working so had booked my train ticket from Woolwich, where my work was, to Stanstead Airport. At the last minute, my boss decided to change Libby and mine's rota giving us the day off. For me not to be questioned by the train authorities, I decided to travel down as far as Liverpool Street Station to board the train there for the airport. I only found out at that point; I could have gone with Libby as she wasn't questioned – better being safe than sorry, I guess?

So, anyway, I finally arrived at the airport and Libby had gone onto the hotel to book us in, and she told me where to go to catch the hotel bus, but upon arriving, I totally got lost, so I had to go into the airport itself and ask. I finally found it and made my way to the Hotel and met up with my new wife.

Unfortunately, after we went to bed, we only got a few hours' sleep due to excited children in the room next to us. Finally, daybreak came, and a bleary-eyed Libby and Damo were off to the airport to check-in as well as to our breakfast and duty-free shopping!

While we were waiting for our flight gate to open, Libby told me that she was so excited as she only went abroad with her parents before us going to Lanzarote, so this was a totally new experience.

The gates opened, and we were allowed to board our plane. Our plane was a Boeing 737-800 flown by Ryanair, an Irish company. The seats were narrow and very hard. On the way over, I wasn't feeling too bright. I ended up vomiting into a sick bag, not to travel sickness, but feeling ill. Fortunately, it didn't last long, and I enjoyed the two weeks.

Talking about landing – when we came into land at Lanzarote[18], on the left side of the plane, we could see the sun-soaked island of Fuerteventura, and on the other side of the plane, we could just see the sun-soaked island of Lanzarote. The island is brown and desolate with white buildings dotted here and there, but in its own way, it's very beautiful. The volcanic mountains tower out of the ground dominating the scenery. The airport is a small airport with one terminal.

Before I take you to the hotel, let me talk to you about the Island. Lanzarote, or 'Lansarote' as the Spanish calls it, is the most northern and eastern island in the Gran Canaries. The Island, like the rest of its family, is autonomous, which means it defends for itself! It is located approximately 125 kilometres (78 miles) off the north coast of Africa and 1,000 kilometres (621 miles) from the Iberian Peninsula. It is covering 845.94 square kilometres (326.62 square miles). This makes the island the fourth largest within the family. It comes after Tenerife and Gran Canaria (I've been to the latter) in the size of its population – a staggering 141,939 inhabitants. The Island's capital is Arrecife, where the airport is.

Once we managed to get out of the Arrivals area, we had to get a coach to the hotel, which was your average coach of the *National Express*®[19] type. This was a bit tricky because I didn't know Spanish, but I had someone with me who learnt the language during her school exams – my amazing new wife, Libby. We were guided to the area where we were able to wait for the bus, only to find that it was delayed. But, no matter, we stood enjoying the warm sun and talking about how we thought the hotel would be. We overheard a typical brit saying, 'I only need to know one Spanish word and it is the word for 'Beer', and that is bière' – yup, that's right, he said it wrong. The drive to the hotel[20] would take us about half-an-hour to an hour to get to it as we had to drop everyone else off at the hotels on route.

When we arrived at our hotel, we weren't expecting it to be ours (I found out later, that Libby had realised it was ours, but didn't want to say anything. I told her that I did too as I saw the name of the hotel).

Upon entering the hotel, we found it very spacious and big. We were welcomed with a warm and welcoming smile by the receptionists who promptly booked us in and then driven around to our room. Yes, I did say '*driven*', and it was in a car! I couldn't believe it. Seriously, think about it – you arrive at a hotel, and the reception says, '*The porter will take you to your room, Mr and Mrs Quinn*' and you hear behind you, the porter saying '*Por favour, señor y señora, sígame. Déjame conseguir tus casos*' and in English '*Please, sir and madam, follow me. Let me get your cases.*' And he leads you to a car, and you and your new wife look at each other, thinking how far this room is? Believe me, it's just pure amazing, and I think both Libby and I were in awe at the whole experience of it.

The hotel had three pools, two adult pools and one pool for children. One of the adult pools had a boat in it which was one of the many restaurants that were in the hotel, and the water of the pool was as warm as the sea – as in not very warm at all. Seriously, if you're a guy and you get into this pool that I've just mentioned, you'll feel your manhood say 'Yeah right, I'm going back inside. Tell me when you're finished in here, and then I'll drop back down!' The other adult pool is where Libby attempted (and succeeded I thought), to do aqua aerobics. I basically stood on the bridge watching her and bopping along to the music! Especially when *Gangnam Style* came on.

The whole of the two weeks was amazing, and we made some lovely friends who will always be on our minds. We were even close to moving to the island to work there, although we had jobs in the UK to deal with.

Ahh, the food…all I can say (and I expect that Libby will agree with me) was heavenly. We mostly ate at a restaurant which did buffet food, and I know that isn't to some people's taste, but we did like it. We did have food, which was very anglicised, but overall it was delicious. If you ever go to H10 Hotel Rubicon Palace, then I'd recommend you try it.

Driving — The Sense of Freedom

I have always wanted to learn to drive since I was legally able to do so, i.e. from the age of 17. Unfortunately, my parents didn't think that I would be able to, also didn't think that I was 'mature enough' to learn to drive.

I decided to put it onto the back burner and wait for a while and gained life experience. It wasn't until after I went to University, where my Mother and I approached the subject again. We made a 'contract' where it said that she would pay for my driving lessons if I got down to a certain level of weight and Libby, my Mother and I signed it.

Unfortunately, I didn't manage to get to the weight and Libby, and I moved to London. But I kept it in mind. When I gained enough money, I went, and house sit for my Dad and looked after the cat called Ginger. I arranged to take driving lessons with a company called Red Driving School. I got a very nice driving instructor, and she took me out for the lessons. Unfortunately, I couldn't finish the lessons as you needed to take the theory exam before you take the practical exam, so I had to wait again before I do the lessons again.

It wasn't long before I was back at my Dad's house doing the house sitting while he was in the States. I booked a series of driving lessons with Red again and took my theory exam and passed it. I finally passed the practical driving exam as well and went back to London with the ability to drive.

Although, I had the license, but no car. While I was working, I signed up to Enterprise Car Club and used their cars to get about. I then gained the inheritance from the death of my Mother, and I bought a car through Autotrader™[21] and Evans Halshaw™[22]. I finally chose the car that I wanted with the help of Libby. It was a VW Golf with 32,000 miles on the clock and only had one owner. I booked a time with Evans Halshaw to go and see it and give it a test run. The car was still in the thoughts of it was its owner who was driving as we went onto a dual carriageway and it was sluggish to get up to 70 miles per hour. But I liked it and bought the car there and then.

Now, I've had it for about three years, and it is used to my driving. If we are on the M11 just before the open speed limit sign, I can get to it, and all the tailgaters behind me are basically eating my dust as the acceleration to 70mph is very quick! We have had a few scrapes together, but that was due to my inexperience of driving. Although when I was on holiday with the group that I featured in the photos, and I will talk about later. I was pulling out of a junction onto a quiet road (luckily), and the minibus that we used to ferry everyone around didn't apply his brakes, or failed, and went into the back of me. I got the car back to the bunkhouse and checked it out and took photos of my bumper, his bumper as well as the reg number. It didn't make me happy as I saw my car hurt and it would cost a lot to repair. Eventually, after a lot of toing and throwing, I sent a request for the insurers to deal with it (as the driver of the bus said that he'd pay for the repair but was not happy with the price of repair) and finally, it was sorted.

Libby had named the car Lexi, and it suits it. I have made changes to it, and it is a good car. The sense of freedom that it gives me is massive. For example, Libby and I can go see my sister in Herefordshire, and we don't have to wait for the trains or find that we can't get a seat. And if we leave our house at like 6 am, we can get there about 8-9 am.

Security Work

Christmas 2014, I was admitted to hospital with breathing problems. In the last section, I said that that I wasn't feeling very well on the flight over to Lanzarote. I was also sick at the hotel. Well, this was the start of my illness which rendered me in hospital.

I woke up one night and found that I was having trouble breathing and Libby instantly got onto the Emergency Services, and I was rushed off to the hospital. They managed to sort out my breathing and then I had to be an in-patient for round about a month while they investigated the cause of the loss of oxygen. They allowed me out in time for my birthday on February 20th. Until May 2015, I was laid up in my house on an oxygen machine and couldn't go far without one. I had more tests and more trips to the hospital for sleep tests as well as other tests.

Eventually, I was fit enough to go back to work, Libby suggested that I should get my door supervisor qualification, as I enjoyed working for G4S at the Olympics as we had decided that the chemicals that were in the pool had made me ill as a colleague had also had to have time in hospital.

So, I found a course in Luton near my parents' home and went I did the course. The course is delivered by Get Licensed (who call themselves as a marketplace for the different courses) on behalf of Security Industry Authority (SIA). It teaches you how to be a door supervisor and the laws that accompanies the job. Recently, I gained my Closed-Circuit Television (CCTV) Public Spaces certification, and there the laws are much more taught, than in the Door Supervision as we are dealing with Data Protection, Human Rights, and much more. But, must admit, I was in my element as I love learning about the Law (I think I can give thanks to my Law colleagues at University. So, once I passed my Door Supervision course (DS), I started looking for a job. I gained an 'ad-hoc' job where I did one shift which was at an Asian Wedding at the Waltham Forest Council buildings. Although, I spent most of the time looking at the beautiful…no, don't be rude…I was going to say – cars…like Lamborghinis, Ferrari, Maserati…etc. Yup, I was in my element once again! I love cars and only can dream about having one of the premium cars that are around. Although, in the UK, these cars aren't suited for the British roads, so they'd just be part of my 10-car garage (although, that number most likely would increase)!! Anyway, I digress…

After this one job and finding out the other jobs listed for this company was only Close Protection (also known as bodyguards) jobs, I decided that I would start looking for another job. I eventually found a job in a company called Kings Security, who did Retail Security. They placed me in a shop that was down in South London and boy, wasn't that scary for a newbie? I was at the shop for about six months to a year – found out that the shoplifters were on a 'conveyer belt' as I call it, meaning one in one out within a matter of minutes. We got all sorts of shoplifters – people who came in on mobility scooters, people who escaped on a pushbike, people who carried knives and guns, etc. This entry to my job of Retail Security was quite dangerous, but I pushed on. Fortunately, over the time I was with them, I managed to gain courage and faced the shoplifters. It did take me a while, but I got there. Now I can safely say that if I ever get a shoplifter in the shop and they get out, I am 'hunting' them down and arresting them. Today, I'm securing Estée Lauder shop, M•A•C™ Cosmetics®. I am based in the heart of the LGBT Village, Soho, which is such an amazing place to work at as I see a whole variety of people at the shop, as well as an odd shoplifter now and then. I would rather see no shoplifters whatsoever, as the law-abiding customers are more interesting than the shoplifters! Anyway, working in Soho is such an amazing experience compared to the last place I worked at, in Stratford (East End, not *William Shakespeare's* home) as there I received rudeness from all sides which didn't make me happy. Now, I dread the call when I have to go over there to fill in as Soho is a million times better. I am hoping that by the time that this book is published, I will be on my way to becoming an Area Manager for the Retail Sector of Mitie within the South East. This job will entail me travelling around the shops that have Mitie officers and see if there are any problems. It will also entail me to travel which I will enjoy (hopefully, my petrol will be paid for as it will be a bit difficult if I can't do the job if I am broken down!)

With that said, I am back studying as I would like to get a higher wage, but I also would like to be in Computing. So, tell me, what do you think I should do? Well, I love security. I love computers and the Internet – so why don't I bring them together? Well, I did, I am currently studying for the job of Cyber Security Analyst, starting with CompTIA A+. Then the next lot of courses will be CompTIA Security+, Net+ Cisco CDN1 and CDN2. This is not an easy subject to do as I already have problems reading books generally. But I am hoping to get there and become a Cyber Security Analyst. In today's world, we are facing a barrage of threats from criminals who want to steal everything and anything from us, companies and governments. So, I'm wanting to join the forces who are trying to protect the UK and its residents from such attacks. More on this later.

In the meantime, I wouldn't mind being a dog security handler, but unfortunately, I need more training for that, and at the moment Libby's and my house isn't big enough, and we have two Bengals (although, I think that they'd make friends with the dog as they are friends with the local foxes!). My favourite dog is the German Shepherd, and I vowed that unless I retire to the countryside with a house that has at least 40+ acres of land, my dog will be a working dog as I live in London!

In my current job, I wouldn't mind becoming a manager of a team, but some days, I get a feeling that you need 5+ years in the Security Industry which is a shame. Although, I have found out recently that I will be able to move up very soon. By the time this book is published, I am probably either starting to become a manager or a fully-fledged manager. Though I always do hope that this book does well, and I get a lot of offers to do talks about the disability. I do enjoy my job but would like it to stretch my mind a lot more, perhaps that is why I opted to do the Cyber Security courses. I feel that if I learn lots, it makes me an all-rounded person and besides, what I'm doing at the moment with the book and the Cyber Security courses is to show that I am able to do I.T. to people who look at me disapproving and think I'm just an idiot and unable to do anything except low paid jobs.

Weekend Away

After a year of having Libby worry about my health problems and her long working hours at the leisure centre, we decided that we should go on a short break to Edinburgh, Scotland, where could just relax and enjoy the sights and sounds of Edinburgh.

I found that Edinburgh had their *Christmas Market* from November to January and we decided that we wanted to see that. I looked up the train fares for the trip up to Scotland and found out that it was more expensive than a flight up, so I managed to get a flight up to Edinburgh, along with an '*add-on*' which was the hotel.

We travelled up to Edinburgh a week after the Paris shootings by the terrorists, so Libby was anxious and so was I, but I managed not to let it show. We touched down in Edinburgh on a chilly Friday morning with the winter sun beaming down on us and glorious blue sky. We were picked up by taxi (also which I booked) and then driven on to our hotel (with a sort of a guided tour). When we arrived, we were met by a concierge who promptly welcomed us and took our cases in to be checked in. Libby and I were again in awe at the look of the hotel. The hotel is an Edwardian hotel which was built in 1905 where it housed *The Scotsman Newspaper,* and later, in 2001, the paper moved to their own purpose-built building, and the building was renovated into the Scotsman Hotel which stands on the North Bridge today.

We could go and get lunch and have a feel of what's about Edinburgh as our room wasn't ready. The city is a very beautiful place, where it is mixed up with the old town and the new town (the New Town was on, if I remember correctly, the hotel's side of North Bridge, and the Old Town, was on the other side).

The Christmas Market runs along Princes Street and St Andrews Square. It is quite a big event with lots of stalls selling a lot of different stuff, from jewellery to coffee. It runs every year and probably could well have over 2,000 people visiting it from all over the country. We had lunch and then went back to the hotel to check-in.

Inside the hotel, it is a big hotel with wood and marble interior and a five-star feel about it. We were shown up to our room after checking in by the concierge who met us when we got out of the taxi. The room was small but very cosy with its own mini-bar, and en-suite bathroom. The view out of the window looked out over the bay (no before you ask, we weren't sitting right on the sea, it was about 15-20 miles away) and we could see Edinburgh Waverley down below us.

The next day, we started our trawling through the Christmas Market for presents for our families. The Christmas Market is quite an extraordinary place; if you ever in Edinburgh around Christmas time, I'd recommend you visit it. The market sold, like I said, anything from jewellery to coffee. They could be really '*in your face*' type of jewellery or delicate types. And then it sold things like Christmas hats and scarves, tourists tack, and handmade items made from wood or metal.

Near St Andrews Square, they had children and adults performing on several stages, admittedly, this was near to the Christmas lights being turned on, but it still was around the Christmas Market. We didn't stop to watch many of them, as at this point, we were sight-seeing.

On the final day, we decided that we should do some 'real touristy stuff' and booked ourselves on a bus tour. The tour took us around Edinburgh, and showed us the following areas of Edinburgh:

- Palace of Holyroodhouse
- Scottish Parliament
- Old Town
- National Museum of Scotland
- Grassmarket
- Edinburgh Castle
- New Town

As we found out, Edinburgh, like a lot of the UK, has a lot of history, and it was quite an interesting tour. If Libby and I go back, we decided that we would go and see the National Museum of Scotland as when we saw it on tour, it sounded interesting as it sounded as if it told the story of how Scotland came about.

CompTIA courses

As I had already mentioned the CompTIA courses, I thought that I should talk to you about them…well, a bit about them.

In the field that I want to go into, Cyber Security, the are several courses to do with CompTIA, and they are:

- **CompTIA A+ 901/902**

  For this one, to get the full certification, you **must** pass both exams. This course will go into the technical aspect of becoming a Computer Technician. It'll teach you everything from ground up and what you should do and shouldn't do. For example, I use to build my own computer, and I mistakenly touched the motherboard without grounding myself first. You probably can guess what happened next if you do any of this kind of thing – I put the motherboard in and finished setting it up, and it didn't work. I was pretty certain that I did ground myself by having an anti-static strap and mat or touching the metal on the computer. So, it could have been just faulty.

- **CompTIA Security+**

  This is the next course in the CompTIA list. This will teach you how all about how to secure your computer, network, etc. I haven't quite got here yet because reading isn't my strong point. But I am trying to do my best to get to this point. The next lot of courses, I won't be saying much about it but will try to give you some information on it. CompTIA says for this course:

  - CompTIA Security+ is the first security certification IT professionals should earn. It establishes the core knowledge required of any cybersecurity role and provides a springboard to intermediate-level cybersecurity jobs. Security+ incorporates best practices in hands-on troubleshooting to ensure security professionals have practical security problem-solving skills. Cybersecurity professionals with Security+ know how to address security incidents – not just identify them. (ComTIA, 2014)

- **CompTIA Net+**

  This course, I think, is going to be the hardest. I tried to get my CCNA while at College back in Luton, and I was unsuccessful with that as the reading was a lot and as I've said it's not really my strong point. Anyway, as the name sort of suggests, this module goes into Networking and CompTIA says the following:

- Network+ ensures an IT professional has the knowledge and skills to:

  - Design and implement functional networks
  - Configure, manage, and maintain essential network devices
  - Use devices such as switches and routers to segment network traffic and create resilient networks
  - Identify the benefits and drawbacks of existing network configurations
  - Implement network security, standards, and protocols
  - Troubleshoot network problems
  - Support the creation of virtualised networks (ComTIA, 2014)

- **Cisco CCNA ICND1, Cisco CCNA ICND2**

  These two courses are the last two that I'm doing in this series. These are from the networking giant – Cisco. I can't find at the moment any details on this, but I think it is all about networking with routers, and wireless equipment., like Network+ I'll have to let you know when I get to it!

Now that I've described the courses that I'm doing to become a Cyber Security Analyst, I feel that all of the subjects I am doing in this course, given to me by a UK company called The Training Room, based in Poole, Dorset. I do have to say and will always say it, I do find it a vertical learning curve when it comes to I.T., but I always have my Mother in my head saying, '*Just give it your best shot, darling*', and that is what I'm aiming to do. If I don't, then I could be in a dead-end job for a very long time with very low pay. I don't think that Libby would like that, as I think (or I like to think that she does) she sees potential in me with I.T.

I also feel, even if I don't succeed with all of it, if I can just pass the CompTIA A+ course, I can build a career out of that. It would be good to go back to building my own computer and maybe make it into a gaming computer. Also, another reason for me wanting to be a Computer Analyst is because I think I could be the first person with Developmental Language Disorder to be in this field. How amazing would that be and am I determined? Hell yeah! I am extremely determined. Especially when some people don't even think that I am able to pass it. I have gone what I call – '*radio silent*' (which means in my terms – I don't talk to them) – with those people as they're a bunch of nobodies and not worth my time.

CHAPTER 10

A Newspaper called the Early Times

You can never get all the facts from just one newspaper, and unless you have all the facts, you cannot make proper judgements about what is going on.

—Harry S Truman

OKAY, IT IS ABOUT TIME THAT I DO A BIT MORE MEN-TIONING OF AFASIC AND MY WORK WITH THEM. This one and the next three chapters are all about what I've done to help the charity that is called, Afasic.

Let us start from the beginning of my journey to being a Vice President of Afasic (*see Chapter 12*).

Back in the early 90s, there was a paper which was for children called *The Early Times* (now defunct), and it had a section which was entirely written by people aged between 13 and 17. These people were anyone who could get the newspaper in the age range that was mentioned. It was about anything that they wanted to write, thoughts about their towns, thoughts about trouble in their countries, etc. as the people who were writing for the section were kids from all over the world.

Firstly, I would like to apologize to anyone who has heard me talk before; I hope it doesn't get too boring for you.

I am dysphasic – that means I have a speech and language impairment. In my case, the most obvious symptom is that I talk slowly because I often have to search for the words - and some people don't listen – or perhaps can't be <u>bothered</u> to listen – to what I am attempting to say.

But now it's Christmas, the season of goodwill. So I trust you to lend me your ears and be patient!!

I also, so I'm told, am not good at grammar and sometimes – again I'm told – say things that are not appropriate.
The trouble is that, with both of those things, I don't know when I'm going wrong.

So you have been warned!!!

I'm sure that I speak for most dysphasics when I say that this disability is <u>more than a bit frustrating</u>.

It <u>can</u> be a big embarrassment talking to people – especially on the telephone.

<u>I</u> often can't find the words which I would like, so I end up stuttering across the sentence – or taking ages to finish it.

Then people try to finish it for me. Unfortunately – I am afraid to say – this annoys me – especially as they usually get it wrong!

For some reason, I don't actually remember much about my childhood, but I'm told that I couldn't speak - or understand at all - for quite some time.

Sample of a talk

While I was at Dunstable College, I was practising to become a better touch-typist as they had a piece of software that would time your word per minute, and if you were too slow, it would ask if you were typing with gloves on. I thought about my DLD and how many people didn't know much about it.

So, I decided that I wanted to write a piece about it and what it was like being someone with DLD. I recently found the article again and have put it into the book. I also, found that someone from the BBC wrote to the Editor asking if I could do something for them, but unfortunately, that didn't happen or at least not to my knowledge it didn't.

Once it was published, I showed it to my Mother after reading it myself, and she suggested that I should send it off to Afasic and they asked me to do a talk for them at the Parents Conference, which they hold every September where parents and professionals come and hear speakers and get information on how to support their child, e.g. if the child is in nursery and they're moving up to the next school. I, with my Mother's help, put together a speech that I could give to the parents and professionals. The day came, and we went together to Parents Conference, and after their Annual General Meeting, I got up and stood in front of them very nervous with my Mother in the seats watching me (now, she was the Chair of Afasic), and I started to do the speech. I felt my legs start to shake as if they turned into jelly and felt my hands get clammy with sweat.

As everyone who has done a speech will agree, never mind if you are a beginner or a seasoned speaker, it is never easy. I have heard in interviews, on YouTube that no-one can get away from the fear of doing a speech. Many a seasoned professional, has spoken of their trepidation at performing a speech in front of a live audience.

The American entrepreneur, William Buffet, said that he was so nervous at public speaking that he *"would arrange and choose his college classes to avoid having to get up in front of people"* and now, he's one of America's richest businessmen. For someone who is a DLD, it can be much harder. All types of questions can go through your mind while you are giving the speech; Are they bored? Can they understand me? When will this finish? But I haven't had too many boos or rotten tomatoes thrown at me, so I think I'm doing okay.

Eventually, after I stumbled through the speech, I saw that the audience gave me a standing of ovation and it has given me the sense of thrill to see that I can spread awareness by giving speeches about the disability. These seasoned and professional speakers should now be jealous of me. Anyway, I now take the opportunity to do speeches whenever I can. I have recently spoken at Scala[23] at the Marriott Hotel in Bristol. I was asked by Afasic to go to this dinner presentation for the company who was also fundraising for Afasic. So, I got my speech ready, put it onto the iPad and set off with Libby to go and speak to the members of Scala.

We arrived at this very posh hotel and went up to the receptionist and told her who I was and what I was doing there. The receptionist looked at the computer and looked at me blankly and asked, 'Who are you?' 'Damian, from Afasic' 'Oh yeah, I've found you now. Sorry, sir, it doesn't look as if you have paid' 'Err, the person who created the booking did'. I then promptly phoned the person from Afasic back, and he told me that he did pay, and I passed the phone over for him to sort it out. Fortunately, it was finally sorted after an hour, and we were shown to our room.

The room was very swanky and nice. Libby set about taking the freebies from the room! But, if you go to a posh hotel, that would have to happen! Anyway, we got changed and headed down to meet everyone else and sat at the table. What we didn't know was that we could have come earlier and used the health suite, like spa, massage and Jacuzzi, as all the wives of the men at the fundraiser all had used the Marriott's facilities. But overall, we were happy to be there.

The time of my talk came; I got up with my iPad and walked up to the podium and switched on my iPad. It was time for a facepalm moment as the iPad literally took forever to come on. I must have gone as red as a tomato as I was so embarrassed by it. Once, I managed to get it up and running, I went on and did the speech and did it successfully. Technology is brilliant, but always have tendencies to let you down at the most vital point!

Once again, the speech was about *Living with DLD* and how I have coped with it.

Another talk that I did, which wasn't so posh as the last one, was at my old school. Yup, that's what I've said. I went back to my old school. Dawn House School was having a Student Participation Conference where, like with the Parents Conference, would have talks from Professionals who help them in the last years of school. They also have students putting on a show for the professionals. Anyway, I created a talk and delivered it in front of the students and professionals. By this stage of my life, I am becoming quite used to speaking, and I am more at ease of public speaking, but I do still have that initial fear of doing it.

I have received so much positive response because of doing the various speeches, that Afasic made me a spokesperson for the charity

I wanted to make sure that I could go further and give more and more speeches. To this day, I have continued to speak for the charity and have been very honoured to speak for them and, for me, it has been a great honour to do so

CHAPTER 11

Spreading Awareness

The first step toward change is awareness.
The second step is acceptance.

—Nathaniel Branden

IN 1999, I DID A SPEECH WHICH WAS IN FRONT OF CHILDREN AT A SCHOOL.

This speech was more nerve-wracking (if that is the right phrase) than the last because it was in front of a group of kids of all ages, but fortunately, they were all pleasant and enjoyed the talk.

Here is the story how I got this talk. I did a talk for the Afasic Parents' Conference as mentioned in the last chapter and after a few days, the CEO at the time, Norma, called me up and asked if I would do a talk for a school. I accepted and started work on my talk with the help of my Mother. I thought about what I could talk about, and we decided as I was going to talk to school children, the talk should be related to them. So, I wrote down everything that happened to me while growing up, like going to a special school, having friends, etc.

Then the day of the talk came, and I made my way down to London and to the school, which was the International School at Finchley. Norma also arrived at the school, and we were shown into the hall where I was going to do the talk. While we waited, Norma chatted to the headmistress about Afasic and its work, and I just stood around revising for my talk. I was very nervous and was hoping that everything would go smoothly. Then we heard the loud noise as all the children piled into the hall. Fear tapped me on the shoulder and spoke to me, 'Want me near you?'

I had to talk to an audience of about 200 children, including teachers. For a first proper talk which was not in front of anyone who knew me, like at the Afasic Parents Conference, it was a bit daunting. The first person to go up was the Headmistress to introduce Norma and myself, then Norma went up and spoke about who we were and what the charity was about.

Then it was my turn. With sweaty palms and jelly legs, I stood up and made my way to the podium. I had all eyes looking at me, and I could feel the thoughts going silently amongst my audience. Will I be able to get through one paragraph without panicking or stuttering? Will I manage to remember my Mother's teachings how to speak to a group of people? I drew in a breath and breathed out and uttered the first paragraph of my talk: "*Hello everybody. It's good to be here talking to you today. But I'm afraid you are going to have to be a bit patient because talking isn't very easy for me. That's because I am dysphasic.*" I looked up and saw that I captivated everyone. I continued to the end and received a raucous applause from the school and a big smile from Norma.

With all the talks that I did, my mother helped me with it and edited it for grammar. I even read it to her as practice. This was due to having to do a lot of talks for NAMM (*See Chapter 3*). It was a great help to me.

Spreading awareness of a lesser-known disability, such as DLD, is very difficult when people decide that there are lots of names for it. Look at all the other disabilities – there's only one name for it, for example, dyslexia, autism, etc. While with mine, there are many names for it. I feel that this disability should only have one name, and I hope that it has been found within the name of 'DLD'. Fortunately, with the hard work that Afasic has put in, along with other organisations, such as ICAN and Communication Trust, just to name a couple and Vice Presidents like myself, the professionals are starting to gain interest. I am hoping that this book can also spread awareness, not just with professionals, but with the parents of possible DLD children and mainstream parents.

Whenever Afasic needed a spokesperson, I was there carrying the torch for them. I enjoy doing the talks now, but do find it hard and at times scary, but I manage. I would love to do talks at TED[74] but that maybe sometime in the future.

But anyway, like with a lot of things in life, spreading awareness isn't easy. It's easy to go to a dinner do, or an event to talk about DLD and raise money for Afasic, but once the audience leaves the event, the next day they'll forget what DLD is. How are we going to keep DLD in people's minds? That's anyone guesses. Afasic is working hard to change that, but it's a steep hill when governments (never mind who's in power, they all do it) make cutbacks in expenses to the charities.

Afasic is only a small charity, and with there being no famous people who have DLD, (as far as I know, never know, I may become the first famous person with DLD) unlike the Dyslexia world, it is hard to gain ground to combat this problem. We have our army of volunteers and researchers who work hard at spreading awareness, but they only can do so much. The volunteers raise money for Afasic, but it isn't enough for the charity to help everyone who needs help. The researchers try to show that the disability is real, and they're succeeding – as you can see from my chapter about DLD (*See Chapter 1: What is DLD*), but more needs to be done. I feel that writing this book and the website that accompanies this book could be just a drop in the ocean, but it may make waves instead of ripples – or at least I hope that it will.

CHAPTER 12

All about Afasic

To communicate is truly a gift. It is a wondrous ability of your amazing human body, the ability that allows us to connect with other humans to give meaning to our lives. I will argue that it is what makes us human."

—Kathleen Depperschmidt

Afasic is a charity that helps a lot of children and young adults with DLD and their families. I will try to show some of the great help that Afasic does for the children, young adults and their families. Let's start with the history...

The History of Afasic

It all began back in 1968 when a Speech and Language therapist was told about a boy who couldn't speak and had the worst temper tantrums that she's seen. This speech therapist would set up an association that would later become known as Afasic, and her name was Margaret Greene. The temper tantrums that the boy was having was through sheer frustration of not being able to speak. The mother of the boy was virtually pulling her hair out as the professionals believed that the boy should be sent to a mental health institution which was very common in those days.

Afasic in the early days (Credit: Afasic)

Margaret Greene says *"It was the general opinion of speech clinics then that it was pointless to refer children for speech therapy before they were of school age. There were no diagnostic facilities; the tests available were very limited, and consequently, many children were being sent to special schools, the general provision did not exist."* (Greene, 1983) So, she decided to set up an association for parents of children with DLD.

At her first meeting, Margaret received a lot of encouragement from two people who were Mr Tony Martin, the director of the Nuffield Speech and Hearing Centre, and Dr Mary Sheridan, who at the time had the responsibility for the deaf and hard of hearing at the Ministry of Health. These two were her rock.

Margaret continues to explain the process "I had been determined from the start that Afasic would be an association for parents. After reading Elizabeth Browning's book (Browning, 1972) *about her own experiences in bringing up a son with severe speech and language difficul-*

ties – the frustrations, lack of understanding and ignorance she and her family faced – I knew she would be the ideal person to join the committee of Afasic and take responsibility for publicity and fundraising." (Greene, 1983)

Margaret Greene died in 2007 and will always be remembered in the hearts and minds of people who have worked for Afasic or with her. The legacy that she and Elizabeth Browning forged still lives on within the Afasic Family.

Present Day Afasic

It's been 50 years since Margaret Green and Elizabeth Browning started up Afasic, and a lot has happened. No-one can expect a charity to become big overnight, as it takes a lot of hard work. Afasic isn't big, it's not even international, but it has a big heart and tirelessly works to awaken our society about DLD and how difficult it is for the children and young adults who have it. And 2018 marks their *50th Anniversary*.

At the centre of the work that Afasic does is fundraising. Like with all charities, they need to get money from somewhere, and fundraising is the best way. The charity holds a lot of a different kind of fundraising, from coast to coast bike ride (I'll come onto that in a bit), to running in the Virgin Money London Marathon, from being silent for 24 hours, to singing loudly at Christmas. The Christmas Carols is featured in Chapter 12. So, what is 'Being silent for 24 hours'? Well, it's also known as 'Zip it for Afasic' where you are silent for 24 hours…basically *'what it says on the tin'* as the saying goes. Several people now have completed it and have raised a lot of money for Afasic.

I feel that if people know more about the work that Afasic does, then better the help that they can give to people like me. At the moment, people who know about this charity are the people 'who are in the know', like people with children who have DLD and the health professionals. Unfortunately, like I said, the charity doesn't have very much money, and with Brexit looming over the UK's head, it's struggling, so it is unable to do big marketing campaigns, such TV advertising, billboards advertising, etc.

If I had the money, I'd get them to help me with a marketing campaign where it is all the above suggestion, and maybe it'll be able to promote them to the top spot! But seriously, how do you get a small charity to become well known? By having everyone talking about it. Well, I'm hoping that this is the start and will give Afasic a big boost to getting more people talking. Also, it must be something which people know about. In the UK, the largest charity is Gavi Fund which raises funds for Child Vaccines. Why do you think this is the largest charity? It is because that they show children who haven't been vaccinated and pull at the heartstrings to make people donate money. This is all fair, and I agree with it, but my work is with Afasic. How can you show people who have DLD and get people donating? It isn't easy, because the difficulty is hidden and is only noticeable when the DLD person start to talk.

The steps to this are as follows:

- Get a DLD to write his or her autobiography;
- Get the book to be in the bestseller list, by word of mouth, and very good marketing campaigns;
- Get people talking about the disability;
- Get the author of the book to do tours of the country to speak to companies, schools, colleges, health departments, etc. about the disability
- Get mainstream companies to donate money to Afasic, and to hire people with DLD

The only problem with these steps is that it is difficult to get it started. But as I am someone with DLD and writing an autobiography, it is a start.

If I could wish for one thing, it is that my disability gets noticed and kids who have it and getting born with it, mainstream people know how to deal with it. And also, governments will spend millions on getting people trained up as Speech Therapists and building schools like Dawn House, Moor House, and Meath School, the three special schools which accommodate children with DLD.

Afasic Bike Ride

This is probably the most fitness powered fundraising that Afasic has. I did it back in 2003, and I rode along with some other people, including Mark, the Director of Fundraising, from Avonmouth, Bristol, to Yarmouth, Isle of Wight.

As aforementioned, we started off in Avonmouth, near Bristol. I was taken to the place by my Mother where we met up with the group and started off on our long hike to the final destination – Yarmouth in Isle of Wight. What we would encounter was more than any person could face. It was about 145 miles and would take us about three days. We faced rain, hot and dry sunny days and for me, a date in the hospital.

So, we set off about 4 pm in the afternoon of a Friday and the day started off bleak and cold like if Death was touching us with His cold finger. Eventually, it brightened up, and our hearts were lifted, and we got into the mindset of this long and difficult bike ride. The first bit of the journey was quite easy, with just a few rolling hills. It wasn't until we got into Day 2 of our ride when things got difficult. Here we had more hills and a lot tougher ground, but fortunately, my Mountain bike could manage it with ease. During the day, we stopped off for lunches, and in the evening, we slept over in a school that was Afasic's books.

Unfortunately, on Day 2, I only got as far as Salisbury as I fell off my bike and ended up in the hospital due to a broken shoulder. How did it happen? Well, we were coming down a hill and what I saw as I turned a corner was a straight road.

Around the corner which was hidden came an old Golf and I managed to avoid it, and then came a Mini, or what I call it, a BMW Mini. I applied my brakes, no, not 'brakes', but 'brake' – the front brake – and I went straight over the handlebars and slammed into the tarmac with a bone-crunching thud and slid about 5 yards across the road. When I finally came to a stop, there was a lot of swearing until I realised that the driver of the Mini was behind me, asking me if how I was. I managed to respond to him, and the rest of the team arrived and looked after me. I found that I had a painful shoulder which I couldn't move and a very bloodied bicep. One of the team washed out the wound while another phoned the driver of the support minibus to get them to return to our location. The bloodied wound which I had, every time someone poured the water over it to wash it out as I had some of the tarmac in it, it would continue to bleed profusely.

Finally, I was ready for the support minibus to take me to the local hospital while the other riders continued to the next stop-off point. I was an outpatient in Salisbury Hospital A&E (Accident and Emergency) and had my shoulder prodded and believe me that was very painful. The wound was patched up, and I was placed into a sling.

I returned to the team as I wanted to finish the ride with them (albeit, within the confines of the minibus as I was told by the hospital that I couldn't ride for a while). We all finally arrived in Yarmouth,

For anyone who likes biking and would like to raise money for Afasic, I'd recommend it (but just don't fall off your bike, as I did. I don't recommend that as it hurts!). Since when I did it, they have been virtually all over the country – including the UK's four nations – Scotland, Northern Ireland, Wales and England (where they finished at the Headquarters).

Through the bike rides and the other fundraising events, members have raised a lot of money for Afasic."

Afasic's Work

So, that's the fundraising part, what else does Afasic do? Well, the charity puts hours and hours of research and work to show what DLD does. Some of the papers that were used in the earlier chapters (*Chapter 1: What is DLD?*) were written by Afasic, or the CEO, Linda Lascelles.

Afasic is the founding member of The Communication Trust, that supports children and young people that struggle with the everyday task of communicating, due to them having DLD. Like with what I've said in this book, communication is the key to getting through our lives and living it to the full. Look around you; everyone is communicating in some way or another, even if it is in sign, it is still a form of communication. Children and young adults with DLD, find it hard to express what they need, what they need to play with, what they need to learn.

Along with Afasic, BT, the Council for Disabled Children, and ICAN, the Communication Trust was formed to help children and young adults gain the ability to communicate.

Here in the UK, over *1 million children and young adults* have some form of long-term speech, language and communication difficulty (worldwide, it is estimated that it is 3.6 million children (Collins, et al., 2017)). Just think about it, that 2-3 in every UK classroom. In poor areas, there are over 50% of children that are starting school with delayed communication skills. This means that their speech may be unclear, the range of vocabulary is small, and their sentences are almost one-word answers. They also may only understand only simple instructions, like '*Ralph, sit down*'. With the right help, the children will be able to catch up. Seriously, I know that it's upsetting to see, but these are facts and everything I have told you in this book, is to make my readers aware of this disability. This is not fiction, there may be a child or young adult in your street with DLD and charities like Afasic, and The Communication Trust can help. Without Afasic, it may be a totally different life for children who have DLD, and even though I've had a lot of speech therapy, I still find it difficult talking to new people.

Brexit and Cutbacks

Unfortunately, like with all small charities, Afasic is seeing a lot of cutbacks from the governments, and with Brexit looming over the UK, the charity is seeing the cutbacks even more now. When the British people voted to leave the European Union (EU) back on June 23rd, 2016, they didn't think that the charities would be hit badly as the EU gave money to the small charities, and I see this with Afasic. With DLD not being all that well-known, it is hard for the charity to gain ground for getting any money to help it support the children and families it has on the books.

The charities, like Afasic, rely on money from the UK Government, the National Lottery and as well as the citizens of the UK and the EU. If the money doesn't come in, then it's very hard for anyone to give services to the people they're helping. I can see this every time that I'm with Afasic, and it is very upsetting for me as I never know how to help them. When a disability is unknown, it is hard for people to register it is real, all they think is 'Oh you're lying there isn't a such disability' and instantly forget about what I've spoken about.

Activity Weeks and New Holidays

I have already touched upon the subject of the Activity Weeks that Afasic did earlier on in the book (*See Chapter 3: Growing Up*), but I haven't really mentioned the holidays that came after Afasic decided to close down the older age group holidays.

Afasic did Activity weeks for children and young adults; the ages ranged from 5-18 years old. I was on one of the holidays, which was quite new. Anyway, they had holidays where children and young adults go and do activities such as swimming in the sea, canoeing, walking, rock climbing, etc. Also, parents could get a respite from their children.

The holidays usually happened over the summer holidays where the children and young adults would get a 6-week holiday from their studies, or if they were working, if they were young adults in jobs, would have their holiday leave starting. It would happen at any venue in the UK, and later, sometimes international (I'll explain about this in a bit).

So, in about January time, we would get the list of where that year's Activity Weeks would be. As I said, it could be anywhere. We would then choose where to go, and if we had friends who also go on the holidays from school or we made friends on the previous year, we would try to make it happen that we joined up with each other on the holidays. I have two friends from school, and I would always try to match the holidays which coincided with them. Unfortunately, for two of the holidays, the match didn't happen.

I mentioned that the holidays were international as well as just UK bound. Well, this was because that two holidays that we went on was in Holland and Disney World in Florida. I didn't go on the Disney World holiday, as it was too expensive, but I did for the Holland trip. For that, we made our way to Sheerness in Suffolk and met up with everyone. We then took the ferry over to Vlissingen in Holland. We were joined by a group of Boy Scouts and Girl Guides who were also staying at our place.

This was where I abseiled unaided for the first time, and one of the links basically cried as she saw the difficulties that I had over the years of me going on these holidays. When I got down, she couldn't stop hugging me (years later, she died in her sleep by a stroke after having a day out walking with her husband. She will always be forever remembered in the hearts of the children and young adults who she helped on the holidays).

After Afasic closed down the holidays for the young adults due to a lack of funding, I created a holiday where I got some of the adults who were on the Afasic holidays with me, and the links and took them to the beautiful part of Wales which is Snowdonia. This holiday was a lot of my Mother's doing, and I regret that she had to do it. But the holiday was a success, and it has continued. For the past ten or so years, we have been in a bunk barn just outside Settle, North Yorkshire.

Unfortunately, the organisers who are creating the holidays are doing the same activities every year. There haven't been any new ones for a few years, and they're always asking me what I would like to do about a month before. I give my answer, and when it comes to the holiday, my ideas (or Libby's) hasn't been considered.

The overall price has been slashed too, and the 'Accountant' (who's one of the DLD's father) always says that he doesn't know how the leader has managed to keep the price so low. Libby and I usually look at each other knowingly.

Anyway, it is for the people who do enjoy this kind of thing, and I mostly go to see my friends and put on a poker face.

CHAPTER 13

Vice President of Afasic

The art of communication is the language of leadership.

—JAMES HUMES

IN OCTOBER 2010, WHEN I WAS AT UNIVERSITY, I received a call from the current CEO, Linda Lascelles, to tell me that the chair would be phoning me in a few days, and she couldn't tell me why. When Mike Clifford (the Chairman of Afasic) phoned me, he told me that he would like to make me a Vice President and would announce it at the Parents Conference. On November 10, 2010, it was announced that I was the new Vice President and I was absolutely delighted that I was given a chance to continue my work for Afasic and I was the first Vice President of Afasic who has DLD. And 18 years later, I am still a Vice President and still working hard to spread awareness and enjoying it thoroughly.

I found it funny that I had always looked at the list of names on Afasic website who were Vice President, and thought "*Nah, I won't ever be a Vice President as they're either famous or have worked with Afasic in some way or another*" and now, I'm a Vice President. I couldn't believe it.

Once again, I vowed that I would become the best Vice President that they had and worked hard to spread awareness for them. Being a Vice President is fun, but very hard work and I always trying to find ways of improving the awareness.

Despite having the name — Vice President — on the website, what do I do? Well, being a Vice President is an important job. We must attend any of the events that Afasic puts on and spread awareness. I have been spreading awareness for quite some time, and yet, I feel if I have the title behind me, it gives me some importance to what I'm talking about. I am in regular meetings with the CEO to catch up with what's going on within my charity and help wherever I can.

In November 2013, I was invited to go to an evening dinner over in Bristol, where an architectural organisation called *Scala*. The organisation allowed the members to raise money for a charity, and for the past few years, it was the same charity which I can't remember, but this year, the vote was for Afasic.

I was called by the Director of Afasic England, Tony, who asked if I'd be willing to do a talk for the company, which I eagerly agreed to. I enjoy trying to spread awareness – maybe it's because I'm giving something back to Afasic when they've helped my family and me for the past 41 years. I asked if Libby could come, and this was her first time that she heard me speak at an event.

So, Libby and I headed down to Bristol to do the talk for the company and to be a representative of the charity.

We were staying at the Marriot Hotel, and when we arrived, we found out that the Hotel had lost our booking. This didn't go down very well back at HQ, and Libby was thinking 'Don't you know who he is? He's the star of the show!' Finally, through a lot of phone calls, we were booked in.

The Hotel was quite big with a lot of corridors going off the reception, built with a Gothic feel. It was built in 1863 by WH Hawtin adjacent to the Cathedral of Bristol. Our room was medium-sized but cosy with an en-suite bathroom and a four-poster bed. Here we got ready for the evening show!

When we were ready for the show, we went down and met up with the organiser of the awards night, and the person who suggested that Afasic should be this year's Charity of the Year. We were asked to sit down at our tables and Libby, and I started chatting to people who were at our table. After a while, Libby leant over to me and told me that we should have got there earlier as the wives had been to the spa facility. Had we known; we would have been there!

Then it came to the time of my speech. I picked up my iPad and went over to the podium and turned it on. With technology, they seem to have a brain of their own – they either mess around with you if you're a beginner, or they'll behave when they know that you know your stuff – with the iPad, it just was having a down day as it took ages to come on!

Finally, after about 10 minutes, it turned on, and I started the speech. I stammered through the speech and got laughs and nods from my audience, so I guess that I got it right. About thirty minutes, I finished the speech, I went back to my seat (after having a photograph taken of me) and then the appraisals started to come in. Another speech that went well. I don't think Libby stopped hugging me for some time afterwards! She was very proud of me, despite the glitch from the iPad!

Christmas Carols

Ahh, the time of the year when people get ready for Christmas and put on Christmas Carols. And Afasic is no different. Biannually, Afasic puts on a Christmas Concert and invites distinguished guests and Vice Presidents. And two years ago, in December 2015, they, being Afasic, decided to have a compère which consisted of me, and two other DLD adults called Justin and Kelly.

As a famous author, Mark Twain once said, *"Against the assault of laughter, nothing can stand."* I enjoy watching people falling as they're laughing at jokes told by a comedian. It is a joy to be able to take people away from their daily troubles and turmoil through comedy. And with being chosen to compère, I wanted to see if I could make the Christmas Concert enjoyable for the audience and with my two partners, we made it so successful that Afasic asked us back in December 2018.

Kelly, Justin and I are hosting the Christmas Concert every two years now! (Credit: Greg Keeling)

So, for the second year running, we managed to get through the Christmas concert without a hitch and then we listened to the comments of the concert coming in. Robert Meadmore (an actor and singer for the Musical Theatre) said "*…that in my opinion the Afasic concert really is the best Christmas concert in town!*". The Christmas concert is also a fundraising event for Afasic, and through it, we do raise a fair amount of money for Afasic. It is another way for Afasic to sell their Christmas Cards. You're able to get the Christmas cards from their website around the period. I may be a bit biased here, but I think buying the Christmas cards are worth buying as they do have some very nice designs, and the money goes to a good cause. Even though I'm bringing laughter into the concert; I don't think that my Mother would be impressed. I remembered doing a talk at the Carol Concert and started improvising, and she said afterwards that I was trying too hard. She told me earlier on in the day, she wouldn't be there and came unknown to me. I don't think I uttered a word of a joke since then until now. I hope that she's pleased with this book and everything that I've done in my life since her death.

The church that the concert was held in, is St Andrew's Church which is on the north-western edge of the City of London in Holborn. In 1666, the church was lucky to be saved from the Great Fire of London due to a last-minute wind change, but it was in so in need of repair that Sir Wren said that he'd rebuild it (Various, St Andrew Church, Holborn, 2015).

The church is quite a big building with a high ceiling, and above the entrance, it has it's an organ. Back in the early 2000s, there were Roman artefacts found in the crypt. So, the church even has quite a lot of history!

Radio Interview

On December 13, 2015, I was on the radio in my Vice President role.

A local radio station called *BBC Three Counties Radio* in Bedfordshire, covering the counties — Beds, Bucks and Herts — phoned Afasic up asking them if they had anyone who'd be willing to interview with them, and Afasic thought of me.

So, there I was, making a trip to the radio's studio for a pre-recording a few days before the broadcast date that I just mentioned. I couldn't believe that I was on the radio. What should I say? Must mention about Afasic; my role as Vice President; my school; my wife and her help with Afasic; my autobiography…

Did I say any of that? No, because of the questions that were getting bombarded at me, and the station had time restraints. Also, I ended up very nervous because people would hear how I spoke. But I did manage to get a lot of interesting points across.

At the time of the interview, I was shown into a small, dark studio where the presenters were sat. The studio consisted of a table, four mics and something that looked like a mixing desk where the lead presenter worked her magic for the listeners to be able to hear us. It had a big red light in the centre of the table which lit up whenever we were recording. There was a window to my left that showed another studio where the presenter was droning on about some topic or another, and behind me, there were the producers who were recording the interview.

In the interview, I had someone who managed to control his stammer as well as someone who developed a program which the stammerer went on called *The McGuire Programme* that helps people with stutters to control it. We also had a mother of a speech-impaired child as well as a speech therapist. I thought that the interview went very well.

As I was on while *The McGuire Programme* was being talked about, maybe I should say a bit about it. The programme was developed in 1994 by Dave McGuire after 45 years of having a stutter which had debilitating effects. He found a way of coping with it by using Costal Breathing, which is a type of breathing that is used by opera singers, plus a traditional way of a psychological approach called 'non-avoidance'. Together along with the teaching, this method teaches the person with the stutter how to cope with it. Judging by the person whom I was interviewed with, it works very well. Today, the programme operates in several countries all over the world as far as New Zealand.

I was asked about my life, what DLD meant to me, and how I managed with it. I did manage to talk a bit about my school.

YouTube Video

In 2015, Afasic decided that they should create a series of YouTube videos for their channel which had young adults speaking about their disability and how it affects them. I was speaking as a Vice President, and as a person who had DLD. The videos were created by the boyfriend of Director of Fundraising's daughter who had just recently graduated from the University of Portsmouth studying Media.

It took him about six months to gather up all the videos and edit them. They are all featured on the Afasic YouTube page, which can be found by simply searching "Afasic[25]" on YouTube, and if you'd like to see mine, it's on my website[26].

It all started with Linda getting in touch with me and asking me if I would like to be in a video. She then explained why it was being done. They wanted a series where members of Afasic who had DLD would talk about their difficulties as well as their successes in life.

Little old me was the first person to be filmed, and I set a format of what to speak about.

In the video, I spoke about my time with Afasic, growing up with DLD (at the time of filming, I was calling it Dysphasia as DLD wasn't really used by anyone as it was still being debated by RALLI. That came after once the filming was finished) and my future.

Other children and young adults spoke along the same lines, and after it was finished, Afasic marketed it like anything. The videos managed to get quite a lot of views (especially mine!)

CHAPTER 14

Future Thoughts

The past cannot be changed. The future is yet in your power.

So, here I am almost halfway through my life, and I have completed so much, and still, have a lot to do before my time is up. The future is always changing, and so are my prospects.

My life has been quite an eventful one, and it's been quite a roller-coaster ride. I'm sure that it's the same with everyone, there have been the ups — working for Afasic, gaining the friends that I got at university — and there have been the downs — my Mother dying, getting kicked out of university…but, it all helped me in the long-run. I will continue to hope that I will get some more ups and downs in my life (more '*ups*' than '*downs*' though).

The biggest highlight that I have in my life, well two to be precise, is becoming the Vice President of Afasic and marrying Libby[27].

So, what is the future bringing me? Well, I am hoping to have a fulfilling future where I can do more talks, but at the moment, I have my door supervision badge and am working in security. I still want to work as a Security Dog Handler (this is difficult as the training for it is slim on the ground, so I think that I'll wait for my country house) or in Cyber Security. My favourite dog is the German Shepherd, and I vowed that unless I retire to the countryside with a house that has at least 40+ acres of land, my dog will be a working dog as I live in London! I would love to move to Derbyshire, Somerset, or Herefordshire for the beautiful scenery, ability to go on long walks, and just to be able to get some fresh air! I am also currently studying for the job of Cyber Security Analyst, starting with CompTIA A+. Then the next lot of courses will be: CompTIA Security+, Net+ Cisco CDN1 and CDN2. Hopefully, I'll pass all of them

Away from jobs, I will continue to spread awareness of my disability and Afasic. This part of my life, I enjoy it because I am teaching people like you, the reader, what goes on inside my little brain give you some appreciation of how it feels. It isn't easy when I don't know myself. Ever seen a diagram of the Internet? It looks like it is, well, chaos to put it bluntly! Well, that's what is going on inside my head. I have no organisation and half of the stuff that the brain is meant to retain is erased. Basically, I try to find something in my memories and all I get is an error message saying 'File not find or has been moved'. It can be annoying but, hey such as life! Afasic needs all the help that it can get, either by people volunteering for them or from donations.

Learning is a big part of any human lifespan; even animals learn, and that's why I will never stop learning.

I have told you in the autobiography that I have failed my degree, and even though it has given me the skills, in fact, let me rephrase that — quite a lot of skills, I do kick myself for failing — mainly because my Mother and father were disappointed with me, I don't think my Mother was happy with me even when she died – she pushed me away when she was in hospital and called out for my brother (Libby says that she thinks that my Mother was pleased with me and she knew that I was there, but to this day, I don't think that this is the case. I think she didn't want me there; I don't think that she would be bothered if I didn't turn up) – he is more important in my parents' eyes than me and always has been, hence me never mentioning him until now. So, I have taken it upon myself to do everything to change that. Therefore, I have several big books that I'm working through to make my web development skills a lot better than it has been in the past.

With my website, I would love to see it getting a lot of traffic, even maybe some awards! I am now, taking my time to learn the stuff that I need to know to make it end up being perfect. Not an easy job with someone who has a language difficulty, but I'll get there. With that said, I am always learning, and I will be adding new things as I go through my life. I will continue updating and making it better. I think that now, yes, it's good but it could be a lot better, and that comes with experience and also having content to add to it.

Like I said just moments ago, I want to get lots of traffic as well as maybe awards, but I would rather see people always coming back to it and the website earning me money. I believe that if the website is updated regularly and is interesting enough, then I can't see why it can't have people returning. Like with this book, if it is interesting enough, then people will buy it if it isn't, then it'll just sit on a shelf gathering dust, and no-one will be aware of this disability. That is the same with the site. I could give the site to a psychologist to create, but what is the point of that? It won't be personal, but if I create it, update it, then it's personal as it's from someone who knows what they're talking about. After all, that's why you've bought this book and why you're looking at my website (I hope). You want to learn about the disability.

At the time of me writing this book, I am still intending on getting my Microsoft Certified Solutions Developer qualification, even though I am going into security. It will be for my benefit, just to show people that I can do web development. I just need to keep going at it and work as hard as anything. I want to go back to university to gain a Computer Sciences degree, but I wouldn't ever be able to afford it. As with many potential mature students, the fees are far too high without some sort of additional income.

Even though I am keen on web development, I wouldn't mind trying to learn some other parts of the I.T. world. I wouldn't mind seeing if I can build my own operating system (OS), but I think that will be quite a way into the future. That'll take a lot of learning, and a lot of investment in books! So, for now, I will try to learn everything that'll make me become a good web developer to get my website a lot better. After I have finished the first module of the MCSD, I want to continue through until I have got all three modules under my belt — HTML 5, CSS3 and JavaScript which I'm doing now, then it'll be ASP.NET MVC4 followed by Azure Cloud Server. After I've completed that, I am thinking of doing some different languages which are to do with web development, such as Angular, PHP, a database of some kind, etc.

Another thing that I would love to happen is to become a 'Sir', as in getting Knighted. I doubt that will happen, as I feel that only famous and the wealthy people get Knighted. I am neither of them, but seriously, I would like that. I have been working for Afasic for… hmm how long has it been now? Oh yeah, 26 years! I can't believe it myself. I started when I just arrived at the college in Dunstable. Wow, I have never looked back. I have done so much for the charity, and as I have previously mentioned, I won't stop doing things for them. I believe that this disability should become as well-known as dyslexia, cerebral palsy or any of the other well-known disabilities, hidden or otherwise. I will fight Afasic's corner with them and will keep doing it until something changes.

Having a disability that is so horrible as mine, I feel that I am on the bottom of the food chain. If I died, no-one would care. Therefore, I write this book, to show that even if you get knocked down, if you get back up, you will be able to soldier on through life and have a good life. It will be hard, and I am not saying 'Look at me, aren't I the best!' as I am not the best. Nowhere near. I have people who don't like me because I wronged them in some way or another, but I have just adapted myself not to repeat the steps that I took for them to hate me. Some of those people still hate me to this day, but I can't do anything about it, I just continue to adapt and leave them in the past. Some are friends with me again now, but I feel that they don't want to know me at times because they remember the past.

Whatever you do, cherish the friends that you have as if they stayed with you through the bad times, they will stay until the day that you die. The friends who have left you, you can forget and leave them where they are as they aren't worth the effort and they can't see you for who you really are. Remember this saying, which I quoted in the Introduction: "*Friends will come, friends will go, but only the true friends will stay*". This is very true. The friends that I have gained or have come back to me are my true friends as they are still with me after seeing my flaws! Nothing is easy when you have DLD, but good can come out of it if you work for it. Every day (and I know that I shouldn't do this), I strive to please whoever I am with. If I am working, the management is the people who I want to please. If I please them, then if I get promotion or move jobs, I will get a good reference and yes, I know, everyone does that, but everyone doesn't have DLD which hinders them to going anywhere in life. If I'm with friends, I am constantly watching myself that I don't say the wrong thing.

Despite all of this, look where I am now? I am a security officer, I am married, I am a Vice President of Afasic, and I have an autobiography written and out on the shelves and on Amazon. This is showing that people who have DLD can have a good life, and although it is hard work to get here, it is not impossible. Work hard at your speech therapy, work hard at school, college, university and your life will be successful. Don't procrastinate like I did, just continue to look ahead, not back.

After writing this autobiography, will I write another book? I don't know, to be honest, anything is possible. This book could become a series of volumes (i.e. this one could be 'Volume 1 of 20' for example) where I update it and add more psychology papers into it as they are turned out. Never know, I could help with the writing of the paper, although that may not happen as I am not a psychologist, unlike the people who I've used in this book and my lovely wife. But anything could be a possibility, and for now, I am just thinking about the outcome of this one for now. My thoughts on the outcome are to see this autobiography in the number 1 spot of the 'Best-Sellers' list, and maybe even a movie being made of the book…or is that a bit far-fetched? Now, yes, I think it is. But I wouldn't say no to the book being made into something — a documentary or something… again, I say this – to raise Afasic's profile. I feel that a documentary would be better than a movie, but I don't think it is possible. Fingers crossed though.

After all of this and saying where I'd like to be after I've published this book and what I hope that I will do in the future, is just a thought, no-one knows where they will be in the future. I wouldn't mind doing the things that I've said, but I may find another track and head down it. It's like a 'Mind map', you start off on one path, and then something else comes along, and you move over to that path, and then you realise after a few months that where you started isn't where you have ended.

We can always hope that what we say now will happen in the future. But, nine out of ten times, it doesn't happen. For now, I will continue down this road and see where it leads to. First step to see how popular this autobiography becomes by publishing it!

All I have got to say now is, thank you for buying my book and I hope that you now will pass on the word about it and make it popular.

The End...or at least for now!

*

References

Afasic. (2004). *Glossary Sheet 3: Development language delay/developmental language disorder.* Farringdon, London: Afasic. Retrieved from http://www.afasic.org.uk/news/free-downloads/

American Psychiatric Association. (2013). Diagnostic and Statistical Manual of Mental Disorders. In *DSM-5* (Vol. 5, pp. 42-44, 50-59). Arlington, USA: American Psychiatric Association.

Autotrader. (2018, August 30). *What do we do - Who we are - Autotrader.* Retrieved from Autotrader: https://plc.autotrader.co.uk/who-we-are/what-we-do/

Bercow, J., Lascelles, L., Beardshaw, V., Daniels, T., Gadhok, K., Lamb, B., . . . Slonims, D. (2008). The Bercow Report. *The Bercow Report*, 21-79.

Bishop, D. (2014). *Ten questions about terminology for children with unexplained language problems.* Oxford: International Journal of Language & Communication Disorders.

Bishop, D. V. (2017). Why is it so hard to reach agreement on terminology? The case of developmental language disorder (DLD). *International Journal of Language & Communication Disorders.*

Bishop, D. V., Snowling, M. J., Thompson, P. A., Greenhalgh, T., & The Catalise-2 Consortium. (2017). *Phase 2 of Catalise: a multinational and multidisciplinary Delphi consesus study of problems with language development: Terminology.* Oxford: The Journal of Child Psychology and Psychiatry.

Bishop, D., Clark, B., Snowling, M., Frazier-Norbury, C., & Conti-Ramsden, G. (2014). *Specific Language Impairment (SLI): The Internet RALLI Campaign To Raise Awareness Of SLI.* London: Psychology of Language and Communication.

Browning, E. (1972). *I Can't See What You're Saying.* London: Paul Elek Books Ltd.

Chief Secretary to the Treasury. (2003). Every Child Matters. *Every Child Matters*, 13-102.

Child and Adolescent Psychiatry. (2003). In D. V. Bishop, M. Rutter, & E. Taylor (Eds.), *Speech and Language Difficulties* (Vol. Fourth, pp. 664-677). Oxford, Oxfordshire, United Kingdom: Blackwell Science Ltd. Retrieved February 12, 2019

Collier, L. (2014). *Walthamstow Through Time*. Stroud: Amberley Publishing.

Collins, P. Y., Pringle, B., Alexander, C., Darmstadt, G. L., Heymann, J., Huebner, G., . . . Zindel, M. (2017, September 18). *Global services and support for children with developmental delays and disabilities: Bridging research and policy gaps*. Retrieved from Plos: Medicine: https://journals.plos.org/plosmedicine/article?id=10.1371/journal. pmed.1002393

ComTIA. (2014, May 1). *CompTIA Security+ Certification*. Retrieved from CompTIA Security+ Certification: https://certification.comptia. org/certifications/security

Conti-Ramsden, G., Botting, N., & Farager, B. (2013). *Psycholinguistic Markers for Speci°c Language Impairment (SLI)*. Manchester: Cambridge University Press.

Conti-Ramsden, G., Mok, P., Pickles, A., & Durkin, K. (2013). *Adolescents with a history of specific language impairment (SLI): Strengths and difficulties in social, emotional and behavioral functioning*. Manchester: ScienceDirect.

Frazier-Norbury, C., Gooch, D., Wray, C., Baird, G., Charman, T., Simonoff, E., . . . Pickles, A. (2016). *The impact of nonverbal ability on prevalence and clinical presentation of language disorder: evidence from a population study*. London: Journal of Child Psychology.

Gallagher, A. L., & Ebbels, S. H. (2017). Language, Literacy and numeracy outcomes of adolescents with (Developmental) Language Disorder following a collaborative model of SLT delivery in specialist education. *Outcomes for adolescents with Language Disorders*, 3, 5.

Gascoigne, M. (2006). *Supporting children with speech, language and communication needs within integrated children's services*. London: RCSLT. Retrieved from http://www.rcslt.org

Greene, M. (1983). *Afasic – how did it all begin?* Retrieved from Afasic: https://www.afasic.org.uk/about/afasic-how-did-it-all-begin/

ICAN. (2013). *What's it like to have speech, language and communication needs (SLCN)*. Retrieved from Talking Point: http://www.talkingpoint.org.uk/young-people/whats-it-have-speech-language-and-communication-needs-slcn

ICAN. (2015). *I CAN - The children's communication charity*. Retrieved from ICAN: http://www.ican.org.uk

Law, J., Lee, W., Roulstone, S., Wren, Y., Zeng, B., & Lindsay, G. (2010). *'What Works': Interventions for children and young people with speech, language and communication needs*. London: Department of Education.

Mander, D. (2001). *Walthamstow Past*. London: Historical Publications Ltd.

Norbury, C. F., Tomblin, J. B., Afasic, & Bishop, D. V. (2008). *Understanding Development Language Disorders - From Theory to Practice*. Hove, East Sussex and New York, USA: Psychology Press.

Reilly, S., Bishop, D., & Tomblin, B. (2014). *Terminological debate over language impairment in children: forward movement and sticking points*. Oxford: International Journal of Language & Communication Disorders.

Roulstone, Beverley, Lascelles, et al. (2011). *Listening to Children and Young People with Speech, Language and Communication Needs*. Guildford: J&R Press Limited.

Simpson, N. H., Addis, L., Brandler, W. M., Slonims, V., Clark, A., Watson, J., . . . The SLI Consortium. (2013). *Increased prevalence of sex chromosome aneuploidies in specific language impairment and dyslexia*. Oxford: Developmental medicine & child neurology.

United Nations. (2010, October). *Convention on the Rights of people with disabilities*. Retrieved from United Nations - Disabilities; Department Economic and Social Affairs: https://www.un.org/development/desa/disabilities/convention-on-the-rights-of-persons-with-disabilities/article-27-work-and-employment.html

Various. (2014). *About Us*. Retrieved from The Beaucrees: Rockin' 60s Again: http://www.thebeaucrees.co.uk/band/about/

Various. (2015, July 13). *English Civil War*. Retrieved from Wikipedia: https://en.wikipedia.org/wiki/English_Civil_War

Various. (2015, December 9). *St Andrew Church, Holborn*. Retrieved from Wikipedia: https://en.wikipedia.org/wiki/St_Andrew_Holborn_(church)

Various. (2015, July 10). *Walthamstow.* Retrieved from Wikipedia: https://en.wikipedia.org/wiki/Walthamstow

Various. (2015, June 16). *Watling Street.* Retrieved from Wikipedia: https://en.wikipedia.org/wiki/Watling_Street/

Villanueva, P., Nudel, R., Hoischen, A., Angélica-Fernández, M., Simpson, N., Gillissen, C., . . . Newbury, D. F. (2015). *Exome Sequencing in an Admixed Isolated Population Indicates NFXL1 Variants Confer a Risk for Specific Language Impairment.* Los Angeles, USA: PLOS Genetics.

Walker, R., Baker-Bates, C., & Brown, M. (1984). *Story of Leighton Buzzard.* Bedford: Bedfordshire Education Service.

Wilson, A. C., & Bishop, D. V. (2018). *Resounding failure to replicate links between developmental language disorder and cerebral lateralisation.* Oxford: PeerJ.

Winstanley, M., Durkin, K., Webb, R. T., & Conti-Ramsden, G. (2018). *Financial capability and functional financial literacy in young adults with developmental language disorder.* Manchester: Autism & Developmental Language Impairments.

Winstanley, M., Webb, R. T., & Conti-Ramsden, G. (2018). More or less likely to offend? Young adults with a history of identified developmental language disorder. *International Journal of Language & Communication Disorders*, 257-258.

Wray, C., Frazier-Norbury, C., & Alcock, K. (2016). *The Gestural Abilities of Children with Specific Language Impairment.* Lancaster: International Journal of Language & Communications Disorders.

Useful Information

On this page, you will find some useful information for the organisations it you would wish to contact about it you have a child or young person with DLD.

Afasic
http://www.afasic.org.uk

ICAN
http://www.ican.org.uk

Communication Trust
http://www.thecommunicationtrust.org.uk/

1   Under the Milkwood: *http://www.english-literature.uni-bayreuth.de/en/teaching/documents/courses/Dylan-Thomas_Under-Milk-Wood.pdf*

2   With more than 700 years of history, Nottingham Goose Fair is one of Europe's most famous travelling fairs and is still a fantastic event that delights all ages.
    In 2015 the Forest Recreation Ground will once again host over 500 attractions, from the latest white-knuckle experiences, family rides and the old favourites including waltzers, carousels and Hook-a-Duck.
    For thrill-seekers there will be around 100 adult rides and exhibitions.
    (Source: *http://www.nottinghamcity.gov.uk/index.aspx?articleid=23517*)

3   Afasic was founded in 1968 as a parent-led organisation to help children and young people with speech and language impairments and their families. We provide information and training for parents – and professionals – and produce a range of publications. Members meet in local groups in many areas of the UK.
    Afasic seeks to raise awareness and to create better services and provision for children and young people with speech and language impairments. It works in partnership with local and national government, professional and statutory bodies and other voluntary organisations.
    Afasic's mission: Afasic promotes understanding, acceptance, equal opportunities and the inclusion into society of children and young adults with speech and language impairments.

4

5   Virgin Start up is a Virgin company owned by Richard Branson and was started up in 2014. For more information see *https://www.virginstartup.org*

6   This is the flagship document that was published in the UK under a Labour Government between 2001 and 2005. It outlined the needed improvements in care following the untimely death of Victoria Climbie and the subsequent investigations by Lord Laming. The document can be found at: *https://www.gov.uk/government/publications/every-child-matters*

7   Communication Trust - The Communication Trust is a coalition of over 50 not-for-profit organisations.
    Working together we support everyone who works with children and young people in England to support their speech, language and communication.

Our work focuses on supporting children and young people who struggle to communicate because they have speech, language and communication needs (SLCN) as well as supporting all children and young people to communicate to the best of their ability.

We do this because our ability to communicate affects us in every aspect of our lives. Many children could be helped to communicate better, and some children need really focused support to reach their full potential.

No child or young person should be denied that opportunity *http://www.thecommunicationtrust.org.uk/projects/what-works/what/*

[8] Portland College (*http://www.portland.ac.uk/*) is a vibrant national college for people with a wide range of disabilities.

[9] The Tall ships that I went on was organized by Jubilee Sailing Trust (*http://jst.org.uk/*) and their ship was Lord Nelson, the details can be found here: *http://jst.org.uk/our-tall-ships/lord-nelson/*

[10] Linslade Crusaders - *http://www.linsladecrusaders.club/*

[11] Tiddenfoot Leisure Centre - *http://www.1life.co.uk/central-bedfordshire-council/lifestylestiddenfoot/home/*

[12] *http://www.andreaquinn.com/*

[13] Tiddenfoot has two pools, one is a variable based pool that can go down to 3m and is useful for scuba divers and any deep-water activities and a standard 25x12m pool.

[14] HTML is a mark-up language which is the backbone of every website. No websites can work without HTML.

[15] CSS is a stylesheet that makes websites look pretty.

[16] JavaScript is a code language that makes the website do fancy things. For example, back in the 90s, it became notorious due to the pop-up menu. Nowadays, there are much strict rules in what you're able to do with the script.

[17] Vestry House Museum is the local history museum for the London Borough of Waltham Forest, and stands within the village of Church End, Walthamstow. This secluded area still preserves a rural atmosphere, although it lies only a quarter of a mile from Walthamstow's main shopping centre and barely six and a half miles from the City of London.

Vestry House, a two-storey building of brown stock brick, was constructed in 1730 as a workhouse by order of the Walthamstow Vestry. It was later a police station and a private house.

Vestry House Museum is financed by the London Borough of Waltham Forest and since 1931, when it was opened by Sir Ernest Pollock, Master of the Rolls, it has been the borough's museum and local studies library and archive.
The first motor car to be driven in London and the first built in Britain is displayed at the museum. Frederick Bremer built the car in Walthamstow

[18]   For more information about Lanzarote go to: *https://en.wikipedia.org/wiki/Lanzarote*

[19]   National Express is one of the largest coach companies in the UK taking people on holidays or day trips around the country or to the continent.

[20]   For more information about the hotel go to: *https://www.h10hotels.com/en/lanzarote-hotels/h10-rubicon-palace*

[21]   Autotrader is the largest used car selling company in the UK. As they say on their website "From desire, to research, to decision - Auto Trader makes the consumer journey easier.
Our platform offers consumers an unparalleled selection of new and used car listings, enabling them to search from a marketplace of 453,000 used cars and 6,000 virtual new cars each month.
Each advert features a good, great, or low-price indicator, dealer reviews and the ability to perform a free basic vehicle check. We also offer free car valuations and a variety of motoring services and advice to help consumers in their car buying journey.
As 52% of car buyers want to search for their next car by monthly price, we've launched a new finance search tool allowing consumers to search by monthly budget." (Autotrader, 2018). For more information, go to *https://www.autotrader.co.uk/*

[22]   With 130 showrooms across the UK, Evans Halshaw is one of the largest car show rooms in the UK. Here you are able to buy used, nearly new and new cars through their 'Everyday low prices' guarantee. For more information go to *https://www.evanhalshaw.co.uk/*

[23]   Scala is a construction company who annually gives money to charity. At the point of me speaking, they had voted that Afasic should be the 'Charity of the Year' as their chairman was a member of Afasic. More about Scala can be found here: *http://www.scala.org.uk/*

[24]   TED is a worldwide organization which does conferences twice a year where they give talks by top people in their field. It can be in anything, speech, IT, Medicine, etc. For more information, visit *www.ted.com/*

25   Afasic's YouTube page is here: *https://www.youtube.com/channel/UCIV6jk_7XS2wlncNHra9y1w*

26   My website is here: *http://www.dysphasia.co.uk/*

27   Unfortunately, as this book goes to press, after 5 years of being married, Libby and I have separated.

Printed in Great Britain
by Amazon

34813250R00100